MAKING BONES

ALSO BY BOBBY DePALO

Kantfly: A Paraplegic's Story

A Promise

More Promises

The Code

MAKING BONES

THE SEQUEL TO *THE CODE*

BOBBY DePALO

Making Bones

Produced and printed by Stillwater River Publications.

Visit our website at
www.StillwaterPress.com
for more information.

First Stillwater River Publications Edition.

ISBN: 978-1-968548-56-8

1 2 3 4 5 6 7 8 9 10
Written by Bobby DePalo.
Cover and interior book design by Matthew St. Jean.
Cover photograph by stokkete / Adobe Stock.
Edited by Norma Sonstroem.
Published by Stillwater River Publications,
West Warwick, RI, USA.

Publisher's Cataloging-in-Publication
(Provided by Cassidy Cataloguing Services, Inc.)
Names: DePalo, Bobby, author.
Title: Making Bones/ Bobby DePalo.
Description: First Stillwater River Publications edition. | West Warwick, RI, USA : Stillwater River Publications, [2025]
Identifiers: ISBN: 9781968548568
Subjects: LCSH: Organized crime–Rhode Island–Fiction. | Italian American criminals–Rhode Island–Fiction. | Informers–Rhode Island–Fiction. | Murder–Rhode Island–Fiction. | Betrayal–Fiction. | LCGFT: Thrillers (Fiction) | Detective and mystery fiction.
Classification: LCC: PS3604.E6435 C64 2025 | DDC: 813/.6–dc23

I dedicate this book to my godmother.
She is my editor, my muse, my support system.
Thank you, Auntie Norma Sonstroem for your
endless help and unconditional love.

ONE

I sat back in my chair, sipped on more of Grace's brew, and reminisced about my life. I thought I could hear good old "Neighborly-Neighbor" quietly trimming the edges of his lawn with his handheld grass scissors. *I can't forget to bring him home a Nutty Buddy after church tomorrow.*

Some of the more important people in my life are gone now, but all in all, I'm happy. I do miss Carmine though. I miss the old times. Still, after all these years, I can't come into my kitchen without glancing over at the utility closet and imagining dead Carmine jumping out to scare the living shit out of me, with his long nails and boney fingers. It's probably a habit I'll never break out of.

I finished the last drop of coffee from my "World's Greatest Dad" cup, set it in the sink, and made a parting glance at the closet as I passed by the shuttered door.

I thought I heard Grace up by a flushing sound from the bathroom toilet upstairs, so I paused to listen, when out of nowhere, there was a tremendous "Crack!!!" The utility closet's door swung open before me and slammed me hard against the doorjamb! A dark figure in a dark face mask lunged from the closet and shot me in my neck with a thousand-volt stun gun that brought me to the floor in a merciless slam!

The massive number of volts paralyzed my entire being, leaving me laying helplessly and feebly on my back unable to move a muscle, no matter how much I tried!

Puddles of drool filled the corners of my mouth, while sporadic nerve twitches erupted everywhere!

Then the dark figure sat hard on my chest, pulled a scalpel from its back pocket, and removed its facemask.

"Look at me! Look at me!" the culprit demanded—then brutally looked into my eyes, took the glistening blade, and slowly cut my throat from one end of my neck to the other, until a two-inch gash opened up from ear to ear, oozing clots of blood and fluids from my inner self.

"Do you know why I'm doing this to you? Do

you?" I tried to react in some way but I could not move.

Then, using forefinger and thumb, both sides of my cheeks were squeezed tightly together until my lips parted and my mouth opened wide.

"You are a murderer and this is what happens to murderers! Open your mouth! Open It!"

From his shirt pocket, a photograph of Carmine was pulled and put before my eyes for me to see. I still couldn't move. It was then placed over my lips, and the center of the picture was pushed straight back into my drool-filled mouth, and all the way past my teeth, and to the back of my throat! Two fingers kept pressure on it while my eyes opened wider!

Blood gushed from my wound as he screamed ruthlessly close to my face.

"Do you know why?" the unmasked killer waited impatiently for my reply. "Do you?!"

Barely in a whisper, I replied. "Yes. I know why, Nicholas, my dear godson." Then, only mouthing the words, and as my world began to fade away, again, I softly replied.

"I know why."

I then nodded my head before tilting it back while slowly slipping away.

TWO

The smell of Grace's famous brew permeated throughout the house, upstairs and down, still inhabiting the Mancusso home after all these years.

My Heather's fourth grade Father-Daughter Dance picture hung proudly on the refrigerator door, even seven years later—along with Little Carmine's (Sonny's) math quiz and its "Super Job" sticker sadly beginning to dry and curl at the corners.

On the kitchen counter, where Flintstone's Chewable Vitamins once lived, sat Geritol pills, Metamucil tabs, and stool softeners. All with oversized font on each of the perfectly facing labels, lined up in the order in which they are to be used. A somber reminder of days gone by.

And across the cold tile floor, next to the

wide-opened utility closet, lay me, Nicky Mancusso, a Captain in the most powerful crime family in New England and head of this loving household– with my godson and namesake, Nicholas Torro, sitting disgracefully on my chest–with a stun gun pressed against my punctured neck and his two fingers shoved halfway down my throat–forcing a picture of his dad Carmine, past my tonsils, in an attempt to humiliate and punish me for what I had done.

I still couldn't move and began to slip helplessly away, completely paralyzed by a massive stun to my nervous system. My eyes watered heavily and my mouth drooled profusely, like Pavlov's dog.

Oh, and I forgot the most important part. My throat was cut from ear to ear by a scalpel that Nicholas learned to use in a medical program that I had arranged and paid to send him to.

"I want you to know it was me!" Nicholas croaked, through gritted teeth that clenched down tighter than an iron vise.

I just stared back, hard to make out the details of his incensed face because of my tearful eyes and assumed drop in blood pressure. I could taste the acidity of my own blood along with the foreign taste of nasty fingers deep inside my mouth. And the soggy cardboard taste of Carmine's picture? It tasted like shit.

"You made me do this to you! Eat this, eat it!" Tears leaked from Nicholas' eyes as he looked to the ceiling and cried out with raw emotions.

I thought of my children, I thought of Grace, I thought of my .380 strapped to my ankle which had served me so well over the years. But not this time. Not this time!

Nicholas pushed down harder on my chest, jamming his knees into the kitchen floor, while putting more pressure on his dad's photograph, forcing it deeper into my closing esophagus.

The blood from my neck turned to a foam and bubbled in and out as I breathed. I thought of Star and her daughter, Nicki. I've never met the child but imagined she looked like a little china doll, like her mom. Naming Nicki after me was a great honor, a secret I could never share with Grace.

"You will die now! Your throat is cut, and you will bleed to death! Just like a bleating lamb crying for its mama!" I looked back at him without expression. I would not give him that.

The weight of him sitting on my chest seemed to increase as I became weaker and struggled to breathe.

"Do you remember me looking at you during my father's funeral? Did you look into my eyes? I knew. I knew then that you murdered my father! I knew it then and I told you so with my eyes! I told you that you would suffer someday! With my eyes! Do you remember?"

I began to lose consciousness. It was my time.

With blurred vision I focused on his face to stare him down until the end. His image turned to just a silhouette which I locked on as not to give in. If it were only my eyes that kept up the fight, then so be it. I would stare him down in a Mexican standoff. I would surely lose the war but maybe not the battle. Expressionless and defiant, I burned a lasting image of my face into his mind.

See my face and remember it forever, Nicholas! See it in your dreams and see it in your nightmares! I curse you with the image of my defiant, dying face! Forever! I give you the maloik (malawk, evil eye)!

Suddenly, Jesus Christ appeared just behind Nicholas' left shoulder. *Yes! Jesus Christ, the Son of God—He's come to take me to heaven!* I never doubted my destination. Squinting with one eye on my assassin, and the other on my Savior, Jesus came closer into view. I felt elated, euphoric in a sense. God's Son peered over my killer's shoulder to tell me that everything was going to be alright. I could hear Him saying just that, without speaking! And it *was* alright!

As I concentrated on Jesus' loving face, His image began to fade and morph into that of another–and while the lack of blood to my brain initially fooled me, the sudden adrenaline rush awakened my senses and began to reveal His true identity. It wasn't Jesus, it wasn't Him at all! It was... it was my neighbor! Neighborly-Neighbor! Wide-brimmed sun hat, Bermuda shorts, lime-green clogs and all!

Neighborly-Neighbor took his left arm and put my assassin in a most deliberate and forceful headlock. He squeezed my attacker's neck extremely tight and jerked him off of me, while dislodging his fingers from my opened mouth, then planting him face first onto the hard-tiled kitchen floor.

"FBI! You're under arrest!" my neighbor announced, as his air pod dangled from one ear. The other one, obviously a listening device, revealed an ear piece inside of an ear piece. I envisioned him wearing his headgear all those years when he rode his lawn mower, all along thinking it was to keep out the noise while listening to some goofy tunes or something.

"One in custody," he announced, evidently to an open radio mic while cuffing Nicholas like he'd done it a thousand times before.

While placing his handkerchief over my neck wound to slow the bleeding, he spoke again to no one in particular. "This is Deep Impact! I need a rescue at subject 17's address, step it up!"

"Copy that," an unknown voice replied from his earpiece dangling from his neck.

Subject 17? I wondered, coughing up the photograph along with a good-sized clot of blood. *Am I subject 17?*

I began to lose consciousness. The overwhelming urge to sleep was winning as I thought my final thought. *This guy's been conning me for the past seven years? What a stooge I am?* I closed my eyes.

"Oh my God! Nicky!" The shrill in her voice was intense. It was Grace! She was screaming hysterically! "What's happened to you? Oh my God, what's happening? Please no!"

"Please step back, Mrs. Mancusso. Your husband has been severely cut. We have a rescue ienroute."

"Nicky, no! Why is our nephew in handcuffs? Mr. Clayborn, please get your knee off of my nephew's back! Nicky!"

Mr. who? I asked myself, with one eye barely opening. I wondered why I never knew his name. *Did I know that? Mr. Clayborn? Did I know that was his name?*

"He murdered my father! I saw him do it!" Nicholas squirmed with his hands cuffed behind his back, still face-planted on the cold tile floor. "I was on the stairs that morning! He thought I didn't know! I was just a kid but I saw it! I saw it all! It doesn't matter now, because he's going to die! He'll bleed out just like my father did. Just like the pig that he is!"

Grace kneeled on the floor, reciting the Lord's prayer, followed by the Hail Mary, over and over again. The last thing I remember is four FBI agents wearing blue windbreakers with yellow letters whisking Nicholas out the kitchen door, him kicking and screaming all the way.

I totally missed out on the rescue ride to the hospital which was fine by me. Two nurses met the rescue at the back door and worked frantically to keep me alive. As they wheeled me into an operating room on a squeaky-wheeled gurney, they pulled on my arms and pushed on my chest. Way too hard.

One cut my clothes off while the other one hooked me up to all sorts of tubes that I couldn't see. I hoped one was a garden hose full of blood.

I was so doped up I didn't care if they operated on me right there and then without anesthesia. The only thing I didn't like was not knowing if they found the gun I kept hidden and strapped to my ankle. I was a felon, so I was not allowed to have a firearm. But I still needed to protect myself, so I had no choice. Most of my crew were in the same boat.

"Betty, he's got a gun strapped to his leg!" one of the nurses announced quietly, as she removed the cut-up clothing from my body. *Well, that answers that.* I thought.

"Jessie, are you kidding me, honey? He's got a gun?" Nurse Betty spoke as if she were older, but lying flat on my back, I couldn't see either one. "The trauma team is on their way..., be here in a minute or so. Let them deal with the gun, Jessie. Leave it be and finish removing his clothing," Betty ordered. "Hand me the chart, what's the patient's name, honey?"

"Um...it says here his name is Nicholas Mancusso." The one named Jessie sighed, then stuttered a little before speaking again. "Betty, I know him! I know who this man is!"

"Yeah, me too. He's a guy with his throat cut and a gun strapped to his ankle. Come on, hurry up before this room floods with the emergency team."

"No really!" Jessie said. "He helped my dad once a long time ago. I can't...let's put this thing in the storage locker for now, no need to call it in yet..., he has enough problems. Okay, Betty? Maybe he has a permit for it."

"I hope so," Betty replied. "Alright Jessie, but this is on you. I never saw it, understand? I never saw it. Here comes the trauma team now."

Although I couldn't talk, I heard it all. Whoever this nurse Jessie was, she was a standup girl. The team swarmed me like a hive of serious yellow jackets. "Sir! Hang in there! We are going to take good care of you! I understand you have a wife and two children! They are going to want you home safe and sound, so don't you give up, okay?" I couldn't tell which nurse or doctor was which or who was saying what and when. I just knew that I appreciated what they did for me and if I ever made it out of there alive, I'd be forever in their debt. Especially the one who stashed my gun.

I must have passed out again, because I totally missed, um..., September.

THREE

I awoke to the sound and sight of two strangers standing at the foot of my bed. One male and one female. Both FBI. Before acknowledging the agents, I rubbed my eyes while getting my wits together and remembering the events that led up to that moment.

I remembered Carmine's son, Nicholas, jamming a photograph of his dad down my scalpel-slitted throat. Next, I remembered Neighborly-Neighbor—aka Mr. Clayborn—aka "Deep Impact" undercover federal agent, coming to my rescue and saving my hide.

Then there were four days in intensive care after an operation to repair a nicked artery, followed by more miserable days in what I called Alcatraz. Actually, the nurses were great, but the hospital food at St. Mary's Hospital is "*Cagata,*" (a pile of shit-like).

Most ethnicities eat to live; Italians live to eat. We know what's good.

"Hello Mr. Mancusso," said a goofy-looking dude with a bad haircut and too much Brylcreem in his hair. He held out an identification badge with an even goofier picture on it.

"I'm Special Agent Leo Cobb and this is Special Agent Schmitt," pointing quickly to an attractive female agent wearing unattractive attire. "We are from..." I raised both my hands then gave off a wave, still not able to speak much above a whisper."

"Please let me finish, sir. We are from the Federal Bureau of Investigation. We have some questions we'd like you to answer for us. How do you know this man?" he asked, walking towards me and pointing to a photograph of Carmine. It was a little crinkled, so I immediately thought that was the one they plucked from my throat. It wasn't.

"FBI, go away! Please come back another day!" My eyes shifted to the singing culprit standing in the doorway. "FBI, go away! Please come back another day!"

It was one of my crew, Micky Carella, aka Friday Night, looking like a smirk-faced punk kid, still, even at his age. The salt and pepper hair gave him a distinguished look now, giving him even more confidence with the ladies. His wife had to get some work done on her eyes and cheeks just to keep up. Although Friday Night wined and dined his gumadas on Friday Nights, he still made sure he took his wife out to dinner on Saturdays. And as far as the crew was concerned, the family considered him a standup guy.

"Hey Skip, ... uh, Nicky, it's good to see you. How do you feel?"

"Better, pal," I whispered. Thanks for coming. I need you to...,"

"Well, well, well now, what's your name?" Friday said, noticing Agent Schmitt with her small pad and large pencil. Of course, Friday Night had to flirt with the agent. It was in his blood.

At first glance she had the type of look that pegged her as prude, but if you undid the tightly pulled-backed hair and changed the stuffy blazer and man pants, you'd probably reveal a hottie underneath. You usually do.

Friday Night turned to the agent as he walked towards me to kiss my cheek. "Hey, does FBI stand for "Fools-Be-In..., love? Because I am!"

How corny, I thought. But his lines usually worked

for him. Don't ask me why. As I kissed him back, I caught Schmitt trying to look stoic through her blushed face but gave in after Friday Night asked for her first name. "Andrea," she surprisingly replied, which triggered her partner's wrath.

"We know who you are, Micky Carella," said Cobb, sternly. "Or should I call you, Friday Night? An infamous soldier in the Santini crime family. Keeping out of trouble these days? I suggest that you do."

"Me? Keeping out of trouble? Nah, you guys should try it sometime. It would be very liberating for you, especially for a tight ass, piece of..."

"Friday!" I yelled, through a screech and a whisper which hurt to do. "Our new friends were just leaving!" I felt for the bandage on my neck after the outburst and adjusted it even though it didn't need it. "Listen Agents Schmitt and Cobb, anyone who knows me knows that I don't talk to law enforcement without my attorney. But if you want to talk to me about the Red Sox and their pitching staff, I'm all ears."

Cobb led the way to the door. "We will be in touch, Mr. Mancusso."

"Bye, agent buttercup," Friday said to Schmitt

under his breath, as they both passed by his killer looks and boyish grin.

Before they got out of sight, Schmitt, looking down, answered Friday with a whispery, "bye" and got the dirtiest look from agent "tight ass."

After they were out of sight, I held my pointer finger in the air and motioned to Friday not to speak. I pointed to potential listening devices, like, the ceiling fan, the wall clock, the sprinkler head and even the crucifix above my bed.

"In code only," I whispered. He nodded back.

"What do you know about that thing?" I asked.

Translation- "give me an update on Nicholas Torro and the FBI."

Friday shrugged his shoulders and listened for a better clue.

"Did Mrs. Marchetti feed her bird and try to get it to sing?"

Translation- Did the FBI offer to pay Nicholas to testify against the family?

"Because if it does sing you know it will give us a real headache."

Friday nodded and blinked slowly.

"Well, Skipper, we hear that Mrs. Marchetti is giving her bird all kinds of things to eat, but it's a little reluctant to sing. It wants to be able to fly. Mrs. Marchetti is considering it. Letting him fly in return for the songs she wants from him."

Translation- the FBI is paying Nicholas Torro for information but he wants more. He wants to be let free with all charges dropped.

"Get word to the little guy for me," I said. "Also tell the Statue of Liberty guy. See what they think we should do about this bird problem of Mrs. Marchetti's. Maybe the smelly guy can help too."

Translation- tell Santini. Tell the Underboss, Bruno Luccetti too. Ask their advice on Nicholas and the FBI. Also, see if No Neck can get to Nicholas and whack him before he sings.

Bruno Luccetti's nickname was "The Wop," meaning "With-Out-Papers," a term they used as the Italian immigrants passed through Ellis Island in New York Harbor on their way to America. Bruno passed under the Statue of Liberty at the age of five with his mother, grandmother, and two sisters.

"One more thing."

"Yes, Skipper?"

"Mrs. Marchetti's goofy kid. The one that used to like to hang around my house and play in the grass, anyone seen him around?"

Translation- Where's my neighbor? The undercover agent that constantly cut and manicured his lawn while wearing a listening device disguised as music earphones.

"Nah, he's MIA for right now. Must be cutting lawns and listening to his music somewhere else. Those kids go from neighborhood to neighborhood you know."

"Keep on that thing, *capische*?"

"Understood. Will do, Skipper."

"Okay, Friday, thank you for coming. Now go, and be careful." He kissed me goodbye and slipped an envelope under my bedsheet. I never had to ask for tribute money from him. The good soldier he was, he never missed a beat.

A new, second shift nurse marched in with an arm full of white towels and a change of fresh bandages for my neck. She was so new I didn't get to ask her name yet. Of course, Friday Night had to gawk at her on his way out. I'm surprised that's all he did.

"Good afternoon, Mr. Mancusso. I'm Sierra, we haven't been introduced yet..., but hi." She was young. Way too young to be a nurse, I thought.

"Hello Sierra, please call me, Nicky." Filling this

and checking that, she quickly scurried around the room as if she had somewhere else to be.

"Hello, Nicky. It's nice to meet you. On a scale of one to ten, how would you rate your pain level today?"

"Eleven. The neck wound is healing fine but the broken ribs are still just as soar as day one."

"How did you break your ribs?"

"My godson sat on them. Actually, never mind."

"Okay, I'll bring you some Tylenol. Also, I think I saw your wife and daughter signing in at the nurse's station on my way by. Oh, here they are now!"

I repositioned the bandage on my neck as their heels clicked on the tile floor while approaching my open doorway. Just the thought of Grace and my Heather immediately made me smile. Each time they came to see me my heart filled with love for my family. Each and every time.

"Sierra, I want you to meet the love of my life and my beautiful daugh...," I stopped dead in my tracks and tried to pull the words back in as they whispered over my teeth and out my mouth. Because, standing awkwardly in the doorway with nowhere to look but down, stood, not Grace and my Heather, but Star and her daughter Nicki! Yes, of all people. Star and Nicki!

Nurse Sierra must have noticed the silence along with the look on my face. Finally, I spoke.

"Come in, guys!" Star looked amazing. With the same black, bobbed haircut, exotic eyes, and all-around china-doll look, she hadn't changed a bit. Even her clothes were still fashionable and trendy. All that was missing were the stiletto heels and trademark peekaboo star tat on her ankle.

"Um...I thought, I mean this is..." My voice ran out of sound and just emanated breath. "Sierra, these are my friends. This is Star and her daughter Nicki. Star is not my wife."

"I certainly hope not," Grace chuckled, the last one to enter the room behind the two gals, unexpectedly– actually heart stopping, unexpectedly! "If she *is* your wife, you've got a lot of explaining to do," Grace announced, surprising Star and Nicki as she maneuvered past them to claim her territory. By now my pain level was a twelve.

"Well..., uh, I'm going to get that Tylenol for you and I'll be back in a flash," said Sierra. I wanted to escape too.

"Hi ladies, I'm Grace, Nicky's real wife." Grace's

both hands went out simultaneously to greet Star's. She was good like that. As she held Star's hands in a welcoming gesture, I spotted Grace's eyes drop down and then back up again, all in a nanosecond, and in an attempt to size up this beautiful woman she just found in my room being mistaken for my wife.

Grace had on her old Patriots T-shirt and knee-worn jeans. Lots of things went fleeting through my mind–particularly, the words, *this can't be good.*

"Hello, Grace. My name is Star and this is my daughter, Nicki." Grace paused for a second, I think on purpose, before speaking.

"It's nice to meet you, Star. You too Nicki. That's a pretty name kiddo; how do you spell it?"

"It's spelled, N-i-c-k-i."

"How pretty. My husband's name is Nicky too. Just spelled a little differently. Huh. How old are you, Nicki?" Grace wiggled in between them and made her way closer to my side, smiling all the way. *Oh boy,* I thought, *this definitely isn't good*, fidgeting with my television remote and instinctively remembering my .380 usually strapped to my ankle, although I don't know why.

"I'm seven," she answered, smiling at her mom while looking for approval.

Grace continued to smile too, reaching for the box of chocolates on the vanity before offering them each a candy of their choice.

Star began to speak, as she picked out a chocolate with her long, glistening and perfectly-manicured nails. I caught Grace quickly comparing and checking out her own claws. Nails, I mean.

"Oh, by the way, Nicki?" Star asked.

"Yes," both the kid and I answered at the same time. Grace's chin rose up high.

"Oh no, I'm sorry, I was talking to *my* Nicki," Star answered. Grace's chin rose up even higher. "Sweetie," Star turned to the kid. "This is Nicky Mancusso, my good friend. We go way back."

"Hi," the kid said, shyly.

"Hello there, Nicki. It's nice to meet you,“ I said. "And, how have you been, Star?"

"Great, thanks to you." I imagined Grace staring me down but wouldn't look. Nope. "Oh, I have something for you, Nicky."

Star tossed something on my bed, next to my legs. It was a small box, about the size of a brick. I opened it cautiously, thinking that the ten grand I'd given her would have fit nicely inside and would've spilled out, but it didn't. Instead, it held the figurine of a china doll with the shape of a half-moon tattoo painted on its right ankle.

"It's beautiful. Thank you, Star."

"You're welcome. I thought you'd like it. Did you notice the moon tat on the right ankle?"

"I did. It's very nice." All I could picture was an ice pick or knife blade stuck in the right eye of the doll. "How long are the two of you staying in Providence?"

"I wanted to talk to you about that. I heard you're getting out soon. Maybe I could come by the club if I know when you're going to be there?" I still didn't look at Grace and it was tough not to.

"Yes, of course. Just let me clear it with some people first, okay?"

"Okay, thanks." Things got quiet.

"Okay, I'm back!" Sierra blew in like a gust of wind just in time to save the day. "Time for your pain meds!"

Everyone left the hospital shortly after that debacle and all was quiet again. But I'd have to deal with Grace later on, no doubt.

I thought I fell asleep for a few minutes but it must have been hours, because the sunlight outside looked different out the window.

A knock at the door made me jump at first, but I settled down when I noticed the visitor was wearing scrubs. I guess that would be a good way to ice me, because my guard went down when surrounded by people in scrubs. How foolish of me.

"Mr. Mancusso?"

"Yes?"

"My name is Jessie. My friends and family call me Jessie Jayne. Jayne is my middle name. I was one of the nurses in the E.R. when they took you in. Do you remember me?"

"I do. Well, I remember your voice anyway. Come in Jessie Jayne, please. I overheard what you told the other nurse, about secretly taking my ankle holster and pistol off and putting it in a safe place. I want to thank you for what you did for me." I reached out to hold her hand. "I owe you one, Jessie."

She was small, actually tiny, about 5'2". And I'd say she was almost my age, early forties, but the mocha-brown bangs made her look much younger. She had Mediterranean-shaped eyes and full Italian-like lips. Very pretty.

"You're welcome. I told my father what I did, and he said I did the right thing. He said you helped him years ago and was glad I remembered."

"Did I? Who is your father?"

"Vincent Calderone, the stone mason. He used to tell us kids that if it wasn't for you, we wouldn't have had food on our table when we were youngsters. Do you remember him?"

"I'm not sure, please refresh my memory."

"My father said that the company he worked for tried to say that he didn't qualify for health insurance when a cinder block bridge wall collapsed on him at work, shattering his pelvis and spinal column. You have to first follow all safety protocols in order to be covered by accidents.

But Imperial Brick Co. told investigators my dad wasn't wearing his hard hat at the time, disqualifying him from the medical coverage.

"It was true, but the reason he wasn't wearing his safety hat at that second was because he removed it during a moment of silence ceremony that was taking place across the street at the Branch Avenue, Engine 2 Fire Station. They were paying tribute to those six firefighters who lost their lives in the Slatersville Mill fire earlier that week. He had just taken it off when the wall collapsed on him."

"Because Dad was from your neighborhood and

you heard of the story, you went down to the brickyard to speak to the company V.P. on his behalf."

"Witnesses later told my dad that you tried to convince the company executives that a pelvis break on your butt, could not be avoided by wearing a protective helmet on your head. Then, after some push-back, you eventually succeeded by suggesting that the vice president have you insert that hard hat up his *culo* (ass) to demonstrate its lack of effectiveness, after you punched him in his fuckin' head."

"My father says it this way. 'When that bonehead, William Wally, saw Nicky Mancusso coming at him with that hard hat and a tube of axle grease, Wally not only wanted to cover my hospital bills but personally pay for school lunches for all three of my kids while I was out of work.' Jessie paused with sad eyes and a smile. "Do you remember, Mr. Mancusso?"

"William Wally! Yes, I remember him very well! What a stiff! I should have introduced his ass end to that hard hat anyway. So, how is Vincent doing?"

"He's fine but knows ahead of time when it's going to rain. He's happy though just knowing that I was able to help you. Well, anyway–I should get going. It was nice to meet you. Maybe I could come and visit you before you leave the hospital?"

"I'd like that, Jessie Jayne, but only if you call me Nicky."

Tucked in her elastic waist band, she plucked a paper bag from under her smock and handed it over to me.

"Here is your property, sir..., uh, Nicky. And thank you for helping my family."

I began removing my handgun from the crinkled paper bag.

"The pleasure was all mine. And thank you for helping me, Jessie Jayne."

The Walther PPK's stainless steel finish glistened from the fluorescent lights overhead. The .380 isn't the most powerful caliber, but it served me well over the years, and I wouldn't be without it.

While fitting the holster to my ankle, I looked up to catch Jessie eyeing my bare chest through my unbuttoned johnny top. *Another good girl with a bad boy fetish. Been there, done that.* "Now, that's better," I said, cinching the strap through the buckle on the holster. "I felt naked without this thing on. Tell your dad he raised a fine daughter. Thanks again, Jessie Jayne."

"You're welcome, see you soon, Nicky."

FOUR

Doctors and nurses came and went, visitors stayed much too long, days went on and on and all of my flowers were dead. The Italian wandies, Sicilian cannolis, and homemade cookies were all just plates of crumbs, and like them, I was spent. I needed to go home.

Then, the day came where I'd meet with my attorney, John O'Brien, Esq., a big shot lawyer from Boston. I liked the guy and all, but that North Revere accent just made my skin crawl. The way the Boston Irish pronounced their words was like hearing fingernails screeching down a chalkboard.

One day, many years back, I hired him for a court case I had for an IRS thing. I was only 21. Very young. Somehow, he got it transferred out of Providence and to the Commonwealth of Boston.

During the trial, O'Brien said to me, "Mr. Mancusso, for the record, please read back for the court, your statement in the deposition you gave. It's right there in front of you on page 3."

"Sure," I said. "Where is it now? Here it is." I began to read. "Concerning my house in Florida, I had it listed as rental property, yes, but the reason my tax returns never showed any income from it is because my mother and father lived there. My dad wasn't young anymore and suffered from COPD. I wanted to do something nice for them when they turned forty. So, I just charged them whatever the expenses were. Nothing more. It was a wash. I didn't make a nickel on them."

With all eyes and ears listening for my answers, O'Brien continued questioning me on the witness stand in front of Bostonians from the Commonwealth. And here's one for the books.

O'Brien asked a follow-up question like this.

"Mr. Mancusso, was your *mather* fotty?" O'Brien asked, with a straight and lawyerly face.

"What? Excuse me?"

"Your mather, was *she* fotty? In Florida?"

"My mother? Are you kidding me?" I looked at the judge, shifted a little in the witness chair, and smirked an embarrassing smirk. "Am I missing something here, judge?"

"Mr. Mancusso, what's the *praw-blem*, do you understand the question?" the judge asked.

"Not really."

"Why not?"

"Um..., I'm sorry your honor, I don't," shrugging my shoulders at O'Brien then looking back at the judge for help.

The judge was getting annoyed with me, and that kind of pissed me off. Then he rolled his eyes which went right up my ass, sideways.

"Council, please rephrase your question for him, slowly," he said. As if I were stupid.

"Yes, your honor," O'Brien replied. Befuddled.

"Mr. Mancusso, you're .... *mather*, was your *mawm* fotty when she moved to Florida from up *Noth*?"

"Again, excuse me?"

"I'll rephrase. How old was she when she moved to Florida?"

"Forty, I guess."

"So, she was *fotty*, like your dad then, correct?"

Then it finally hit me. *These Boston people don't know how to talk! And I've got the problem*?

"Oh, Christ." I responded. "Learn how to speak English, judge, before you rag on somebody else!"

O'Brien was mad at me for earning a night in the clink for contempt but he got over it.

Today, whenever I remind O'Brien of his goofy Boston accent, he just laughs and says something like this.

"At least I don't speak Rhode Islandeeze and say things like 'I *sore* it last night.'"

O'Brien arrived at my hospital room right on time, with his Armani suit, Trump silk tie, and Tiffany 18 karat gold cufflinks. The shoes were Payless though, not sure why.

"Hello, Nicky."

"Hello, John."

"How are things in *Praw-vidence*? I hear you got yourself in some trouble?"

"Yeah, well, that's why you are here." I pointed to the ceiling light. That meant, "I don't know if we are being bugged or not, so talk in code." O'Brien wasn't Italian, but he sure knew how to speak the lingo when needed.

I asked, "What's the going price of provolone these days? Tell the butcher I'll pay him in all dead presidents."

Translation- How much will it cost me for you to get me out of this mess? I'll pay you in escarole (pronounced *shcarole*, greens, cash under the table).

"That's good, but it depends on how much time is spent on the aging process. I know the butcher is very busy. Is it a big hunk of provolone?"

"It's big. A little bigger than the last hunk I bought a decade ago," I replied.

"Okay, Nicky. Then figure about ten percent more than the last one then, inflation you know. Do you want me to pick you up some?"

"Yes. Right away. Now let me call the nurse, and let's take a 'walk talk.'"

John O'Brien stayed for over two hours, grilling, thinking, plotting, and planning a strategy on what lay ahead if Nicholas Torro cooperated with the Feds.

John kept me out of the can this long, so I had faith in him. When Billy Bath and Johnny Moonlight disappeared, the police tried to pin some involvement on me, and O'Brien got me off. But this was bigger. Much bigger than the last hunk of provolone. The Feds had someone living next door to me for years. Talk about a Donnie Brosco thing! Who *knows* what they heard!

Before O'Brien left, he gave me a gift.

"Open it," he said.

"What's this, John?"

"It's a bug sweep. It detects listening devices wherever you go. Just drop it in your pocket and forget about it. If it detects a bug, it sounds an alarm. You can even set it on vibrate. It's so small, I keep mine on my keychain."

"Really? What will they think of next? Mine's going on my keychain too. Thanks, John."

The last few days in the hospital were busy with therapy in preparation for me to return home, finally.

My strength was back, and I was ready for the outside world again. The news media tried to sneak reporters on the unit, but my loyal nurses always shooed them away.

As for my nurse, Jessie Jayne? She came to see me every night after she got off, and we'd play gin rummy together, then talk about, well...everything.

Grace never knew of my new friend, and she didn't need to. She knew about the club and the girls there and kept her nose clean. She never asked, and I didn't tell.

The hospital set me up with a shrink. They thought that a little throat slitting might bother me mentally, so the doctor ordered it. I tried to fight it, but he said if I didn't go, he couldn't prescribe the pain meds I needed to continue to take for the next few weeks. I figured, what the hell.

Grace came early to pick me up, but the news media came earlier. Channel 10's Calvin Connelly, the guy with the fake hair color and bad comb-over was standing outside the hospital entrance when they wheeled me out.

The boss had another Capo, Jimmy the Weasel, send one of his guys, Ronnie T, to bring a car around to pick me up, keeping my crew out of the camera's eye.

When Johnny Moonlight *disappeared*, Jimmy was promoted to Captain and head of that crew. Being two Captains under *Bruno the wop* Luccetti and Antonio Santini, we needed to get along, so the two of us old-school guys made it happen. I wasn't crazy about him getting his own crew at the time but kept my mouth shut. I guess he's done an okay job.

Mr. Comb-over stuck his mic in my face as soon as my chair's wheels hit the sidewalk. I smelled the fresh bread from DeFusco's Bakery from across the street and realized just how much I missed home.

"Mr. Mancusso, did you have anything to do with

the death of your longtime friend, Carmine Torro, alleged Capo in the Santini crime family? Was the attack on you an act of revenge?" Ronnie T's black SUV was in the right spot, but I couldn't get to it because of the small crowd in front of me.

I shot him a look that said, "Get that thing out of my face," and turned to Grace.

"Honey, let Ronnie T take over." He was way ahead of me and was already removing her hands from the wheelchair.

"Ronnie, push right through." I ordered.

"You got it!"

After running over shoes and jamming leg calves with the front foot supports of the chair, we were at the car in no time. Ronnie turned with arms opened wide, forming an impenetrable wall against the small mob of reporters, while Grace and I hopped in the car behind him.

Pulling away from the hungry leeches, we watched the empty wheelchair roll to the edge of the street, stopping abruptly against the sidewalk and then tipping over on its side, just missing Mr. Comb-over by inches. We headed home.

FIVE

The first morning home was uneventful. Grace had me sit at the kitchen table while she brewed her legendary coffee and set the timer on her twice-baked biscottis. I think she wanted me to get used to that kitchen right away, so I sat there and pretended that I didn't see the discoloration in the floor tiles where pints of my blood stained the floor and the cleaning solution striped the finish.

Being the good husband that I was, I went along and also pretended that I didn't give a damn about the utility closet. Nor did I demand that we seal it up with bricks and mortar until the end of time.

As I watched the steam escape from my mug, I couldn't help but imagine my nephew Nicholas sitting on my chest while I lay paralyzed, beaten and dying on my kitchen floor. The image of my neighbor, an FBI undercover agent, was still fresh in my mind too. I wondered where he was off to these days, probably on a new assignment somewhere. Somewhere warm, as compensation for putting his time in and a job well done.

I was reminded of how I treated Neighborly-Neighbor when he was acting goofy. Grace said he moved out the day after my attack. I know one thing, I admired him for pulling the wool over my eyes for so long. That was a great caper.

Was I worried that they might have had surveillance videos or recordings that could be used in court against the family and me? Nah. They would have used it a long time ago. They had nothing. It was Carmine's kid that I was worried about.

"Today's your first appointment with the psychologist, Nicky. Do you want me to drive you?" Grace never looked up from unloading the dishwasher.

"If I'm gonna get back to the things I did before, I'd better get started. That means driving too. Thank you though."

She looked up with two dishes in her hands.

"Nicky?"

"Yes?"

"Did you kill your best friend, Carmine?"

Holy Shit? I thought, and thought it hard!

I didn't answer back in rhythm—just waited. The question hit me like a ton of bricks, yet deep down I was glad she asked it. Still, I waited, not knowing what to say. And to tell you the truth, I didn't care.

"Nicky?"

"Yeah?"

"I asked you a question. Are you going to answer me?" She stared me down like never before. With eyebrows pursed, she placed the dishes on the counter, took a step towards me, and raised her voice with both hands on her hips.

"Nicky!" she shouted, moving my coffee cup from within my grasp, leaving nothing for me to latch onto. Then there was silence. Silence for as long as I wanted it to be. We both knew that was the most she had. I waited, and waited, and waited.

Then the Italian in me finally spoke. Staring back at her tear-sparkled, green eyes, I enunciated my every word.

"Grace," I said, ever so slowly. "You know not ever to ask me about my work or about my friends. There is a reason for that. A very good reason. You know I'm a somewhat.... powerful man. That much you know. That's all you need to know. So, before I answer you, which I will, I'm going to tell you this only one time. Don't ever ask me about my work or my friends again. Ever."

I reached for my coffee cup, taking any and all remaining power away from Grace.

"As for the question you asked me? I'll answer you this one time, and you'll never ask me something like that again, *capische*?" When I spoke Italian style, she knew I was in Capo mode.

"Did I kill my best friend, Carmine?" I grabbed her arm and pulled her in close. "Look into my eyes as I answer you, Grace. Look deep." I gazed into my wife's trusting eyes and softened mine. Hers began to follow. Slowly, I spoke in a hypnotic and trance-like tone. "The answer to your question is..., no, I did not kill my best friend, Carmine."

"Oh, Nicky," she sobbed, tears flowing fast from both corners of her loving eyes. "I knew it. I knew you didn't do it! She grabbed my hand and rested her head against my forearm, covering my faded tattoo of the Virgin Mary.

"The newspapers said some horrible things that I just knew couldn't be true!"

"They're not, Grace. You know me, I'm not that guy. Now, no more silly talk of this. I need to get ready for my shrink appointment, like I really need that. Will you please iron my dark blue shirt? I'm also meeting a couple of the guys at Helen's Diner for lunch, and I don't want it to show any stains in case I spill something on it - like I usually do. I have to do a few things at the club later on too."

"Of course I will. Thank you, Nicky. Thank you for being honest."

"Always, Grace," I said. "Always."

As I approached my truck, I did my "swoop." Checking under my vehicle was more than just a precaution now, it was a religion. The other habit was to look over at Neighborly-Neighbor's house and maybe walk over and threaten him or bust his chops. But not anymore. I missed that damn undercover agent.

While entering the psychologist's address into my GPS, I felt a sense of weakness and disloyalty to the Family. To my family too. But drove on.

The office building was in a ritzy side of Cranston and had a reserved sign for the shrink in one of the parking spots.

Alex E. Pearlmutter. *Sounds like he's got a stick up his ass. Yeah, I'm sure I'll get along real good with this guy. Can't wait.*

My neck was still itchy from the scar, so I scratched all the way up the elevator ride and into the waiting room. I looked like I'd survived a lynching.

Fancy carpets, fancy furniture, fancy this and fancy that. I did not want to be there.

"I'm here to see Alex Pearlmutter," I said reluctantly, to the over-smiley receptionist at the desk. "My name is Nicholas Mancusso."

"Yes sir, you're right on time! Please have a seat and I'll call your name!"

Call my name? I'm the only one in here! I thought. *I really want to leave.* "Thank you," I said. I sat and waited.

Three or so minutes later, a young woman exited from the inner office area, sobbing as she walked past me and out the door. *Jesus Christ, what did he do to this one?* I wondered.

"Nicholas Mancusso!" the smiling lady announced to the entire waiting room.

I looked around to no one, before raising my hand and answering in an unexcited tone. "That's me."

I was escorted into a large office and told to have a seat. The room was empty when I entered. I took inventory of my surroundings like I always do and noticed there were a thousand places to plant a bug.

The mahogany trim and shelves were dark, giving it the appearance of money. Lots of money.

Nerdy knickknacks were everywhere. So was college junk, along with lots of certificates and diplomas, showing off the guy's accomplishments. I didn't like the "*cafone*" (boasting big shot) already. *I have to do a mandatory six visits with this guy? I'll never make it.* I thought.

Then a quick knock at the door. *Am I supposed to say come in?* I didn't have to, before I knew it there was an overly attractive woman, maybe thirty-five or so, peeking her head in, still holding the doorknob.

"Is it alright to come in?"

"I guess so, you work here, and I don't. I'm just waiting for Pearlmutter," I said.

"Well, I hate to disappoint you, but I'm Pearlmutter. I'm Alexandria Elizabeth Pearlmutter. But you can call me Alex."

I stared back at the shrink, stunned by her beauty. "You know," I replied, "this month has been full of things I didn't see coming. I'm sorry, Alex. I'm Nicholas Mancusso. They call me Nicky."

"It's nice to meet you, Nicky. What brings you here today?" Confused was an understatement, so I didn't answer right away.

She was tall and slender, with delicate shoulders and a slim, streamlined neck below a defined and chiseled jawline. The cheekbones stood out among everything else, and her makeup was impeccable..., oh *Madone* (Mother of God) – her makeup was impeccable. Like she sat in the chair of a makeup artist before greeting the world.

The smokey eye-shadow complimented her cat-like eyeliner which curled up at the corners of her teardrop-shaped, hazel-colored eyes.

The best part of all was her hair. Dirty blond. Dirty blond with even blonder highlights that made the whole package come together. I forced myself to answer her and snap out of the seventh grade, goo-goo-eyed moment I was stuck in.

"What brings me here? Not me, that's for sure. I don't need a shrink," I said, defiantly. "I'm forced to show up for six sessions. The insurance company ordered it and my doctor had to comply. So, here I am." I sat back and scanned the room. "So, where's the couch?"

"What couch, Nicky?"

"The couch I'm supposed to lay down on and tell you my deepest feelings?" Sitting back further, I tested the seat back and cushion. "Actually, this chair is pretty comfy," I said.

"Oh, they threw couches away years ago," she said with a smile. Became too hard to clean the tears and boogers off after each client."

This one's funny, I thought, as she turned the other chair to face me and sat down directly across, making me feel a little anxious.

As she pulled and stretched the hem over her bare knees, I knew that soon, the leg-cross would be coming below that tight slitted pencil skirt. I didn't need any distractions. I loved my wife, Grace, and finally believed that a man was truly a man if he was loyal to his wife. A guy in my position had lots of opportunities to stray, but it can only lead to trouble, and I've done pretty good so far and wanted to keep it that way. *Shit, here comes the leg-cross, I knew it! Look away, look away!*

"Yes, you're right," she continued. "These chairs are pretty good on the tailbone." I pictured hers. "I had one client actually fall asleep while I was talking, drooled all over his Marc Anthony polo shirt. When he woke up, he thought I hypnotized him without his consent! He wanted to sue me! Well, anyway as long as you're here, is there anything you want to talk about, Nicky?"

"Like, what?"

"Like, anything?"

"Um..., let me think." I turned to the bookshelf again and scanned the objects for an idea. There was a picture of a farm with a silo and horses grazing in a field. I thought of Uncle Tony's farm and my best friend Carmine saving me from the electric fence that day. Then I thought of his face years later, asking me, "Why? Why are you slitting my throat?"

I dropped my eyes in a moment of thought. Her legs reminded me of Star's– well, Moon's I mean– the night I sat with her, cold and dead, in Star's Beamer. *Look away!* I thought.

"Well, I do have one question, Alex."

"Go ahead, shoot." Before I spoke, I eyed my bug detector on my key chain to make sure I was protected with my anti-surveillance device. I was.

"My question is this. If someone does something to someone because they deserved it, then later finds out they didn't deserve it, is the person who did the thing to the person off the hook because he didn't know that that person didn't deserve the thing when he did it?"

Alex just stared at me in deep thought, then slowly crossed one leg over the other one and waited some more before she spoke.

"Hmmm..., I think if that someone who did the undeserving thing to the other someone is feeling guilty and remorseful, it may be helpful if that someone talks openly about it to get some closure. Get it off their chest, so to speak. Would you like to tell me what happened, Nicky?"

That was my cue. "Gotta go, Alex," uttering Italian slangs under my breath as I jumped up from my seat and headed for the door. *Vaffanculo...* (fuck off). "It was nice meeting you but I have another appointment. Hope to see you again, and thank you for your time."

"Okay, Nicky– no problem. I'm sorry if I said the wrong thing. How about tomorrow, same time? I'll be more careful, I promise."

I stopped at the door and turned. Her beauty earned her another chance, I guess. "Well..., I guess..., alright. Tomorrow then..., same time. See you then, Alex."

"See you then, Nicky."

SIX

The diner's parking lot was full, so I had to park on the street. Micky Carella, aka Friday Night, waived me on to their table when I entered the 50's style restaurant. It was decorated like the diner in the movie American Graffiti. The walls were covered in 50's memorabilia, and every table against a wall had its own mini juke box you could drop a quarter in.

They were all there, including Antonio Santini, the boss of the family. Bruno Luccetti, the Underboss, and Nunzio Sabatoni, aka No Neck Nunzio sat at the adjoining table. No Neck needed a separate table because of his size, but I didn't bust his hump about it anymore. Everyone else did though. Because he's been around for so long, and probably because no one else wanted it, he kind of earned the unofficial title as the family's acting Consigliere. I can think of worse choices. A guy named Neil Delagatta is really the current Consigliere but he's dying of lung cancer and serving a life sentence. He could and maybe should be replaced but the boss doesn't have the heart to do it.

Meeting my men at the diner was gratifying. One by one, my Crew members paid their respects and welcomed me home. I "made my bones" years ago and should be used to the respect as a "made guy" by now. But I'll never get used to the royalty and loyalty that comes with being a "Made Man" and sitting at the top of the food chain.

"Made Men" don't pay for their drinks, meals, or ladies. The underlings pay and pay and pay, and then long for the day that they may climb the rung to the top.

Friday Night was a good soldier and one of my most trusted and loyal guys. He sat across from me while watching the door. Sitting with your back to the door was bad luck as far as we were concerned, and we avoided it like the plague.

Next to Friday was Mike Tissoni, aka Iron Mike. He was almost as big as No Neck but not as jelly-ish. Legend is, he once punched a guy in the chest, reached right in through the ribs and pulled his heart out before the guy hit the floor. Just a legend, I guess.

Then there was Bobby the Castrator Castratoro. Bobby C. He was an old school enforcer that followed orders without question. He and Friday Night were tight, except Bobby was more of a family guy. I never knew what they had in common. I just knew they would die for one another.

Next to them sat the Sacoccia Brothers– Brandon and Brendon. They weren't rookies anymore but sometimes I still felt as though they weren't wrapped too tight. They were alright though, as long as they did what they were told.

And the two newer guys were just starting to come around, but still had a way to go. They were Tony Canatta and Tommy Gaglione. We called Tony, "Jackpot" and Tommy was just Tommy, unless we called him "gag" but only sometimes. Tony Canatta was smart, good looking and dressed sharp, too sharp, I thought. So, I whispered my concern in Friday Night's ear. Friday nodded once and it was done. The next time I saw Tony he would dress a little down, no question. And, Tommy Gaglione was eager to follow orders too. I was told his faith as a Roman Catholic was paramount, that was cool, but, if he ever wanted to become a Made Man and live by the rules of La Cosa Nostra, he would need to learn that that was paramount over God, family, and life itself. And the Code of Omerta, The Code of Silence, is rule number one. He'll learn... or die trying. That was my Crew and a motley one at that.

Jimmy the Weasel was Capo of the other Crew and showed up late with just a few of his guys. Ronnie T came along with Jimmy Jr, the Weasel's spoiled brat kid that we called Little Weasel. I liked Ronnie T. He was alright, but I couldn't stand Little Weasel. Like father like son. They even dressed the same. Like a sparcone, flashy, showy, God's gift to everyone.

Last to show was an ex-pro boxer named Sonny Nero - him I liked. Why he got into this life, I'll never know. I think that Jimmy conned the hell out of Sonny Nero. Took too many shots to the head maybe, and Jimmy the Weasel took advantage of that. I don't know.

There would be no operational discussions at this meeting, just a get together to celebrate my return and maybe to talk in code a little about this and that.

With a gathering of so many Family members, including Antonio Santini himself, minus some more associate members, of course, the Feds would have had even the salt and pepper shakers bugged. Our faces would be photographed, and government agents could pose as patrons but with long ears and unclean noses. So, on that day it was just ham, eggs and go. No business.

The waitress that Friday called, Dolores Belaruse with the nice caboose, served us brunch but wouldn't even look at Friday Night. She looked madder than a wet hen and knew what he did wrong but we could only imagine.

"Nicky," Don Santini said, his stogie dangling off his right-side corner lip. "How are you feeling? I know you took a hell of a good beating. You okay now?"

"Yeah, I'm okay, Antonio." After the promotion to Capo Regime, he forced me to stop calling him Mr. Santini but I still felt funny about it. So, I avoided calling him anything when I could.

"We need to talk about that thing. Come by the club tomorrow morning, about 7:30. We'll have espresso and some *sfogliatelle* (pronounced *sfool-ya-dell).* You pick them up fresh from the Hill for me. Federal Hill Bakery opens at 7:00 a.m., *capische*?"

Santini then stretched his neck out to see whose plate wasn't empty, for fear someone wasn't eating enough. Antonio was getting up there in age, so I liked spending as much time as possible with the old man.

"*Capische*," I answered back with a genuine smile. It was nice that he wanted to see me, but I knew that an envelope had better accompany that sfogliatelle in the morning. One time I went to see him twice in one week, and don't you know he expected an envelope the second time too? Even if it was lite, he still expected it. Now I've learned to skimp on the green if I knew I'd be seeing him soon after.

Before the senior guys were aware of it, Little Weasel, that snake, was bragging about an insurance scheme he'd been working for the past six months. I'd heard rumors of it but didn't know the details, until that very moment.

"This gig is fool proof!" he crowed, looking down to admire his shiny leather shoes, spotting a blemish, and reaching down to rub it out before continuing. "When this thing takes off, Lloyds of London will never insure another thoroughbred again!"

"*Statazita*!" (shut up) his father Jimmy snapped, but quickly backed off when the old man raised the back of his hand slightly then whispered for him to continue. I wasn't sure what the boss was up to but had enough faith in his wisdom to listen and learn.

"Continue, Little Weasel," I followed up. "That's not a request, continue." His father, Jimmy the Weasel quickly gave me the stink eye but lost the battle just as fast when I gave it right back.

"Well, like I said, this gig is huge! The sky's the limit on the money that can be earned. I buy a young race horse. Nothing talented, just an everyday runner. I throw about two G's for him, not a lot. I insure the shit out of him, like a quarter mill' or something like that. Because he's a race horse rather than a pet, the insurance company isn't the wiser concerning the high policy pay-off.

"This is where it gets fuckin' flawless. I visit my horse every Sunday for one or two weeks. Make it look like I give a shit. When the coast is clear, I take two ping pong balls and shove them up the fuckin' thing's nose. One in each nostril! They fit perfectly! Who knew a horse can't breathe out of his mouth!"

Little Weasel looked down again at his shiny shoes before continuing on. "You gotta fuckin's see it! The horses' eyeballs get so big it looks like they're gonna pop right out of his fuckin' head! His mouth is wide open but no air can get in! He dances around, bangs off the stall's side boards, and looks to me for help in a full-blown panic! It's fuckin, unbelievable!"

"Then, finally, I don't know if his heart stops from a heart attack or he suffocates or if he's just scared shitless! The insurance investigators call it cardiac arrest, that's all *I* know."

Everything became silent. We all just looked and sat there, not knowing if this guy had an actual screw loose or not.

All at once two or three people yelled out, all at the same time.

"Aye! Oh! Aye!" Friday Night jumped up and back, away from the hot pot of coffee that was spilled on his unsuspecting lap! It was Dolores. Dolores Belaruse with the nice caboose! She got him and got him good! "Dolores! Oh!" Friday hollered! She pretended it was an accident but...it was time to go. I drank my coffee down, kissed and thanked everyone for the nice gesture and motioned for Iron Mike to make sure the bill got taken care of. I left the diner thinking about that horse scam and those poor horses suffocating on ping pong balls. *Disgusting,* I thought. *I hope the boss squashes that plan and deals with Little Weasel accordingly. We are not animals,* I thought.

From there I stopped off at St. Mary's Hospital

to see if Jessie Jayne was having her break outside in the statue garden. We liked to play gin rummy by the statue of the Virgin Mary, so I checked there first. I thought we could get in one game before I had to give a guy an estimate on some concrete work and then collect on a few loans I had out. Especially one large one in particular.

I made the mistake of lending a scumbag five grand without knowing that he was also into some New York guys for ten. He was using my money to pay juice on another note. It doesn't work. You will never catch up and I'll get burnt in the end. But he owed me the five grand first, so I wanted my money ahead of those other guys–and I was ready to fight for it.

The scumbag's name was Freddy Luckett. They called him Lucky Luckett, but he was far from that. Lucky was a degenerate gambler that could never quit while he was ahead. If his horse came in to win, say $2500, instead of going home with it, he'd go back to the window and put $2000 on the next race, lose that –and throw his last $500 on a long shot, trying to win back the original $2500.

There she was, eating her gabagoole (capicola) and sharp provolone, with lettuce, tomato, and mustard.

Jessie Jayne and I had become unlikely friends, but it was good. No pressure, no expectations, just easy. After protecting me that day by hiding my gun in the emergency room, I knew that I could count on her. And she me. Friends for life.

Anyway, when she saw me, her face lit up like a Christmas tree. "Ah..., Nicky, you came! I brought you a sandwich just in case. Hungry?"

"Always,"

"Here, try this, it's good."

"Thank you, Jessie."

"Anytime, Nicky. So, what's new?"

"Well, I went to see a.., um... never mind, what's new with you?" Jessie reached down and pulled out a bag of Doritos. You know, the one's that turn your fingers yellow? Although I could have gone for them, there was no way I would allow a Captain in the Santini Crime Family to be caught out in public playing gin rummy by the Virgin Mary with yellow fingers. If I got whacked right there, I'd of been found in a weak and embarrassing position.

"Okay...?" she said in the tone of a question, as if appeasing me. "As for me? Hmm, not much. I saw my lawyer this morning."

"Yor lawyer? For what?" I asked.

Looking down at the pickles sticking out of her sandwich, she slowly answered. "I uh..., well, I may as well just say it. I feel close enough to you now. I was assaulted about six months ago... when walking to my car after a night shift at the hospital." She pushed the pickle back into her sandwich and sighed a big sigh. "They caught the guy and I picked him out of a lineup and all, but his lawyer has been delaying the trial, I think to drag it out long enough that maybe I'll give up and not testify. But I'm not going to be intimidated, Nicky. The trial starts soon and I'm ready to face him."

"What? Are you kidding me? You got assaulted, Jessie?"

"Yes, he left me with this," pointing at a pale mark contrasting with her olive skin on her left wrist. "It's a scar to remind me of the wire tie he used to subdue me after holding chloroform over my nose and mouth until I passed out. When I came to, I had this wrist wound with an emotional scar even bigger than that."

"I don't know what to say, Jessie. Who did it to you?" Her eyes began filling up as she reached for her pickle-soaked napkin to blot her eyes,

"He's an upstanding citizen on the city council

believe it or not, a lawyer– Woody Woodrow Getz, the family man you see on all the billboards during election time. He's a shrewdie. A real con man. Has lots of money too. The cops have been onto him for a while now, but he always hires the best legal team, and they get him out of trouble and keep him out of jail. He's been leaving his DNA all over the place, including on me. I'm not his first." She looked down and away but I could still see the twinkle of tears in her eyes.

"What did your attorney say to you today?"

"He said that Getz claims that all his victims had sex with him voluntarily. And when I get called to the witness stand, his lawyers will try to make me wish I never filed charges. His legal dream team doesn't lose; they find loopholes. Want some cantaloupe, Nicky? I cut extra in case you came."

I just sat there, seething. "I don't know what to say, Jessie."

"About the cantaloupe?"

"About this Getz guy. Is he from Providence?"

"North Providence. You know that brick mansion-looking house on Fruit Hill and Douglas? The one with the two lion statues at the gate?"

"I think I may have seen it once. That's his?"

"Yup."

I saw red! My phone started ringing but I ignored it. "Did he hurt you, Jessie?" She pushed away the last remaining chunk of cantaloupe in her plate, put her plastic fork down and sat back to wipe the corners of her mouth, then eyes.

"He hurt me," she replied, dropping her eyelids and inhaling deeply. Then, she looked up at me through her blurred vision while batting her eyelids faster than the wings of a hummingbird.

With blood boiling, I glanced down at my phone and saw it was Jimmy the Weasel, the Capo of the other crew. "I... I gotta take this, Jessie. Please hang on a second."

"Hello?"

"It's me."

"Yeah?"

"I thought you'd want to know. Those two New York guys? They got your customer. The one that's behind."

"Where?"

"In the back of that guy's thing. The guy with the big nose." That meant, guys from another family had a guy that I loaned money to in the back of Simonelli's chainsaw shop. Simonelli's nose wasn't *that* big, but we had nothing else on the guy, so when you wanted to talk in code about Simonelli, his nose was it.

"I'll be right there. Thanks."

Big nose was with us, so I was pissed that he would let those guys use his place and without my permission too.

As I dialed Iron Mike, I watched Jessie Jayne flick the straw on her juice box. She was in deep thought.

"Hello, Mikey? It's me. Get a couple of guys and meet me in the front of that shop, the guy with the big nose, now."

"Okay, Skipper, on my way."

"Jessie, I have to go. Can we talk more about that thing another time?"

"Yeah, sure, Nicky. I didn't mean to overhear, but please be careful."

"I will."

I made it to Simonelli's in less than 15 minutes. Iron Mike pulled in right behind me and so did Friday night and Bobby Castratoro, aka Bobby C.

"I don't want to start a war over this!" I yelled, waving them on to follow me into the front of the store. Big Nose was standing there looking nervous.

"Simonelli, you piece of shit, you let two guys from out of town come in here and tell you what to do? You don't call me?"

"I'm sorry, Nicky. I was sharpening someone's chain and they just barged right in with Lucky and didn't give me a choice! I did text Jimmy, though! That was good right?"

"Where are they?"

"In the back room, where I fix the chainsaws. Can I go home? I got a stomachache."

"Go."

I motioned for Iron Mike and Bobby C to follow me to the back where we were stopped by two large steel doors. There was no lock to be seen so that was good.

As we quietly stopped about four feet from the door, we heard a high-pitched squeal that... that just didn't sound human! My guys just looked at each other in disbelief!

I'd heard that sound before! It was when that sick cop, Lt. Bergle, had our underboss Billy Bath in his grips as he tortured him then sawed his poor head off! The sound was just as sickening.

Brandon and Brendon showed up and came

rushing in behind us, quiet and controlled. No longer rookies, they weren't so dumb anymore.

"Open these doors, Mike," I ordered. He complied.

"Stand back, Skipper. Bobby, get the other door while I pull on this one." Another high-pitched squeal erupted the second the doors opened, masking any rusty-hinge sound the old doors might have made. We were suddenly inside.

The first room was empty, except for a few open crates that overflowed with chainsaw pieces and parts. The squealing sound continued. One of the Sacoccia brothers put a finger in one of his ears to block out the hair-raising sound!

Bobby moved ahead of us with his semi-auto by his side. He pointed to a corner that was in sight, letting us know that our targets were just around it. He motioned for Iron Mike to go first. I followed with the Sacoccia brothers just behind me.

As we rounded the corner all hell broke loose! Both New York guys ran to the workbenches for something to whack us with. One grabbed a pipe wrench while the other grabbed an ax handle.

Bobby lunged toward them with his nine-millimeter pointed straight out in front of him, keeping it straight out until he was right on them. He hollered,

"Don't move another inch or I'll blow both your fuckin' heads off!" Bobby the Castrator moved right in with the same authority.

"Okay! Okay!" The large stocky one yelled back, throwing the ax handle on the floor..., hard! The tall skinny one watched and followed suit, throwing his pipe wrench down too but not as hard. You could tell he had lots to say but decided against it. He moved about in place like a druggy on a street corner.

The big one finally spoke. "What the fuck, do you guys know who the fuck we are?"

"I know who you are," Bobby replied. "You're a dumb shit from New York that got lost and wandered into Providence where you don't belong. Doing business in another family's town will get you killed, or worse, don't you know that?"

Bobby showed the skinny one the gun-barrel opening and made a sicko-type look on his face while tilting the gun from right to left and then back again. "Don't move a muscle or I'll shoot your tongue. Just the tip off. Try eating Lobster Fra Diavolo without a tongue tip. Ha! Trust me, the stinging pain will be intense and you'll slobber the spicy sauce all over your nice Armani suit."

"Skipper, you'd better come and see this!" hollered

Brandon from somewhere out of view. Everyone turned to the corner of the room that wasn't lit while Bobby C still kept his piece trained on Dumb and Dumber. Brandon pulled the light chain, and the bulb illuminated the area like an interrogation room. We didn't expect to see what we saw next.

There, in the poorly lit corner of Big Nose's damp and cold backroom, sat the degenerate gambler, Lucky Luckett. He sat upon a greasy metal chair with his hands tied tightly behind his back. A strand of barbed wire cut deep into his wrists, while dark red blood dripped on the cement floor.

His butt was planted firmly on the seat, but he was leaning extremely forward. A cautious step forward revealed the most sickening and repulsive sight. His head was secured firmly between two steel jaws with steel teeth of an old steel vice!

Iron Mike approached Lucky and kneeled down to see his face within the tight clutches of the archaic devise. Suddenly Iron Mike leaned back and stink-eyed the two New York punishers.

"Jesus Christ, Skipper, the vise jaws are pressing down on his cheek bones, really hard!" Just then, Lucky squealed again with a nerve racking shrill that made the hairs on my neck stand straight up! Mike jumped in place–then settled down and bent over further for a better look.

"Aw..., no..., you sick bastards!" Iron Mike yelled, still not looking away from the horror! "You sick bastards! Skipper! They popped his friggin' eye out! They tightened the vice down on his head so tight, it pushed his eye out of its socket! What the hell! It's dangling there by a piece of stringy meat! Aw..., come on you fuckin' guys! You sick fucks! And look, Skipper! Skipper! He's still alive!"

Bobby pushed the muzzle of the nine-millimeter in the skinny guy's eye. "Let's put this one's head in the vise and pop one of his pretty blue eyes out, so I can give it to my kid for their marble collection! Then we'll do fatso's!"

"I'm all for that!" Iron Mike replied. Then Bobby pushed the muzzle of his gun deeper into skinny guy's eye. "Just give the word, Skipper!"

"No!" I said. "No, we're not gonna squeeze nobody's eye out. Pat them down real good for weapons, then take them outside and let them go for tonight. I'm not starting a war over this."

I took another look at Lucky. His eye was really just hanging there. Hanging there because they did literally pop his eye out by squeezing his head in that vice.

Broken cheek and facial bones were pushed in and protruded out where they didn't belong. What a sight.

"Wait," I said, placing my hand on Lucky's shoulder. "Bring them here before you send them packing." My crew brought the two of them before me, as if I were to pass death sentences on them. But I didn't. I couldn't. That's why I'm a Captain. Never stupid. I decided to appeal to their senses instead.

"What are your names?" They both looked away, but Bobby stuck the gun-barrel to the temple of the fat one.

"Who the fuck are you, the Lone Ranger?" asked the fat one.

Bobby pressed harder on his temple.

"They call me Mountain and this is Crazy Carlo. And you guys made the biggest mistakes of your lives tonight. You'll pay."

Mountain had one of the biggest heads I'd ever seen, and it probably wouldn't fit in the vice even if Bobby wanted it to. I'll bet I could have fit a whole tangerine up just one of his giant, hair-protruding nostrils. The skin on Mountain's face was covered in bumps too. I didn't know if they were tumors or polyps or cysts or ingrown pimples. I just knew he was butt ugly and his personality didn't help his cause either. He was wider than two men standing side by side and had less of a neck than our own, No Neck.

In fact, his shoulders were higher than his chin, making him look like one of those monsters in that cartoon, Monster Inc.

"You guys will pay!" said fatso.

"Watch your mouth, there, ass-boil," Bobby C replied, pressing the muzzle harder against Mountain's squishy temple.

"You're the first one I'm coming back for," that big oaf boasted back. But he looked silly with Bobby holding all the cards.

"One by one you'll meet your own misery. And you?" pointing to Bobby, "I've got something special planned just for you! I'm thinking, buckwheats."

The skinny guy yelled out while dancing in place. It was almost like he had to pee really bad. *He was the one that flew over the cuckoo's nest,* I thought. "Buckwheats! Yeah, that's it! Buckwheats!" he hollered.

Skinny guy, Crazy Carlo, certainly lived up to his name. *He* epitomized crazy, I thought. One eye looked straight on, while the other looked up and to the right, bringing the word cockeyed to mind. He seemed wired and nervous too. Like a guy that acts on impulse only. Everyone knows the type.

Trying not to act like an animal, I decided to reason with these guys and defuse the situation. As I got older, I tried using mindful methods when negotiating, as opposed to physical tactics. So, I pointed to Lucky and calmly explained that he was a family man that had a gambling problem. A problem that had to be recognized and dealt with accordingly and not with extremes.

With shit-eating grins on both their ugly mugs, they pretended to listen but the smirks remained.

"I'm going to step up here," I said. Tell your boss to respect the boundaries and stay out of Providence. I'll make good on Lucky's loan to you. He's mine now. Then you'll leave and never come back unless invited, *capische*?"

They both nodded, still wearing that shit-eating grin across their foul and obnoxious faces. I looked away, then back at fat and skinny one more time. Again, that grin. As I walked away and headed for the exit, I could still see it in my mind. I briefly closed my eyes, and still, the grin.

"Mikey, take them out and have them wait outside for a minute." I waited until they were out of earshot before I continued speaking. "Bobby, come here."

"Yes, Skipper?"

"Bobby, drop those two "chooches" (*ciuccio*, donkey, ass) off at the Cat for a few hours. Let them drink, eat, lap dances, anything, and as much as they want. Put it on my tab. I'll send over an envelope containing five grand later on to cover the note for Lucky. When you hand it over, you'll tell them to shove it up their asses. Then you'll escort them to the Connecticut border and face them in the direction of New York."

"But before you let them go, you'll wire tie their hands behind their backs, make them open their mouths wide and bite down on the metal guardrail on RT 95. Then have Iron Mike take his size 14 Mondo boots and stomp on the backs of their heads, grinding their teeth into the heavy gaged, galvanized steel guardrail. Then, bag and bring their broken teeth to Lucky, if he lives. What is the rule? An eye for an eye? No, it is an eye for a bag of teeth?"

"I'll be happy to, Skipper," Bobby replied!

"We need to send a message. Don't fuck with Rhode Island, ever. Brendon and Brandon, take Lucky over to St. Mary's Hospital and have them do what they can for him. Tell them he got run over by a car when crossing the street. It was a hit and run."

"*Capische*?"

"*Capische*," they replied.

SEVEN

The next morning, I lay in bed for an extra hour, just thinking. Thinking about the Nicholas Torro thing and about spending the rest of my life in prison.

Grace called me downstairs for coffee and eggs while I was thinking of Jessie Jayne, so I immediately felt guilty. *I gotta get over this thing. I'm feeling like I did when I was a young and stupid soldier.*

Being a wise guy, I had women thrown at me 24/7. Especially by the dancers at the club. That's when I got in trouble and almost lost Grace. *Be strong, don't let it happen again. Be a real man,* I told myself.

I bounced into the kitchen a little too perky, waiting for Grace to ask the first question. But she didn't! She seemed to be engrossed in making my breakfast, the way I liked it. Her head was down, totally immersed in perfecting my cheesy eggs, just the way I liked them.

I dodged a bullet, I thought, pouring half-and-half in my first coffee of the day.

"Who's Star, Nicky?"

Shit.

She turned her back to me to make toast on the kitchen counter and dropped two pieces in and pushed the toaster button down gently.

I thought I was home free.

"Who is she, Nicky?"–spinning around with a slab of margarine on the butter knife, this time looking at me straight in the eye.

"*Ah vaffanculo*!" (pronounced *fongool!* Fuck off, among other meanings, this is the nicer one). "Grace! Why do you do this? You know it's my job! I sometimes have to help people, that's who I am! *Ah fanabla*! Grace! That's what I do and you know this! We've been all through this, and I finally thought it was behind us! *Ah fanabla*!" (go to Naples).

"Nicholas Francis Mancusso! Don't you swear at me, you horse's behind!" her voice cracking. "Who do you think you are? If my father were alive to hear you curse at me like that, he'd wash your mouth out with soap, you...you...you big bully!"

"I'm sorry, Grace, I am. I'm so very sorry." With my head hung low, I reached for both her hands and gently held them, lightly rubbing her palms with my thumbs.

"I don't know what came over me, Grace. I don't... maybe it's the Nicholas Torro thing. You know, I loved that kid like a son. The attack really messed with me, Grace, honey. That's why I need you to be understanding, sweetheart. Okay?" I kept massaging her palms with my thumbs, speaking softly and reassuring.

"Why is her daughter named Nicki?"

"Aw come on, Grace! Jesus Christ!" I said, dropping her hand. That must have ticked her off, because her eyes changed to a look I knew very well. Like when I was a kid, and I had just got caught stealing a pack of cigarettes in Martino's Market. Old man Martino shot me a look like he was going to take my head off. Then when the cop got there, *he* shot me a look like *he* was going to take my head off. Then, when my old man got me home, and with that same look, he *took* my friggin' head off.

"I'm out of here! No questions, remember, Grace?"

"This is different," she screamed.

"Goodbye, Grace!" I spun around, disguising the

walk of shame with anger instead. It worked. In my mind anyway.

I made a parting glance at the utility closet, as I barged out of the kitchen. I imagined someone hiding in there, permanently, peering through the shutters with a window into my family's life. I felt embarrassed as to what they just saw.

Arriving at the shrink's office pissed me off right away. There was nowhere to park except for the empty space with the 'Reserved for Dr. Pearlmutter' sign on it. I wanted to get out, break it off its pole, and bring it in with me to my appointment after parking there.

Just before I finished with my little fantasy, a lipstick-red Porsche 911 zipped into the space like the car was on autopilot. It landed with the exact amount of space between the sexy little car and the yellow lines on each side of it.

Just as fast and with a fluid motion, Alex exited the car, left leg first, wearing another high slit pencil skirt that opened all the way to kingdom come. *Don't look, look away!* I pulled away from the spot before she saw me and parked on the street in a no parking zone.

The overly-happy receptionist greeted me like we hadn't seen each other since high school, or in my case, reform school. Then, just like the last time, she checked me in, had me take a seat, opened the waiting room door, called my name, and waited as I looked around to no one else in the room.

"Mr. Mancusso?" *This chick's a trip.*

I raised my hand and was escorted into the doctor's office and told she'd be right in. *Yeah, I know what that means.*

Ten long minutes or more went by before a knock was at the door, just like the last time. *What is it with these college grads?* I answered in the form of a question. "Come in?" *Why do they knock at their own door?* I thought.

The door opened and there she was, even more stunning than the last time. *Keep your eyes up! Don't look anywhere but in her soft, hazel eyes!*

"Hi Nicky, how are you? Was that you I saw in the parking lot?"

"No, uh, I mean yes. Um...I'm fine uh, Alex. How are you?" *God, she's beautiful.*

"Well, honestly, I've been better," Alex replied. She sat across from me crossing one leg over the other.

Why, what's wrong?"

"My Porsche was broken into Friday night while

parked behind Mama's Restaurant on The Hill. They took my purse which was in the glovebox. License, credit cards, they can all be replaced, but my mother's locket was in there. I was taking it to the jewelers on Saturday to fix the broken clasp. I'm heartbroken over this. The locket was given to Mom by my grandmother and contained a picture of her and my grandfather on their wedding day. I haven't told my mom about it yet because she's going in for bypass surgery next week. It'll devastate her, totally devastate her. Well, enough about me. What's new with you, Nicky?"

"Do me a favor, Alex. Don't tell your mother about it yet. Give me a couple of days to see what I can do."

"What do you mean?"

"Just give me some time to reach out to a few fences."

"Is this what you do, Nicky? Are you involved in stealing people's lockets?"

"Not exactly," I chuckled. "Do you not know who I am?" She crossed her left leg over her right and sat back in her chair, forgetting to pull her skirt's hemline down to cover her exposed thigh.

"Evidently not. What I do know is that you were mandated to come here by your doctor and not really thrilled about the six visits they imposed on you. I get that. I also remember the question that you had for me concerning someone other than you. You wanted to know, and I'll quote, "If someone does something to someone because they deserved it, then later finds out they didn't deserve it, is the person who *did* the thing to the person "off the hook" because he didn't know that the person didn't deserve the thing when he did it?" "How'd I do?"

I couldn't take my eyes off her. *How the hell is she able to help guys with this huge distraction invading the conversation all the time?* "You did pretty good, Alex. Very good, actually."

"Thanks, do you want to tell me what this person did to the innocent victim? It sounds like the perpetrator is guilt-ridden and needs to get lots off his chest." I leaned back and crossed my arms.

"How about we do this, Nicky. Let's call your friend who did the undeserving thing to the other person, um...let's call him, Matt Damon. And let's call the person that Matt Damon did the undeserving thing to... how about, Ben Affleck? Sound good?" Her smile extenuated her beauty even more. "Why don't you tell me the story of Matt and Ben?"

It was hard to say no to this creature. Maybe

that was her scam. Like the girls at the club. They knew how to work the guys to get what they wanted. I wanted to prove that what I did to Carmine was justified, so I played her game.

"Okay, Alex. I'll play. In my world we call the game–talking in code." I sat forward in my seat and uncrossed my arms.

I briefly thought of my PPK in my ankle holster, looking for a security blanket, I guess.

After that, I looked to the door behind her, which was closed. Then finally, I scanned the countless hiding places a bug could be planted by my new friends, Special Agents Leo Cobb and Andrea Schmitt. But my bug detector didn't go off, so I relaxed a little. "Okay, Alex. Where do I begin?"

"At the beginning. What did Matt do to Ben?"

"He offed him."

"He what him?"

"He offed him. Popped, wasted, whacked."

"Oh."

"Surprised?"

"Yes."

"Do you still want to do this, Alex?"

"I do. Why did Matt *whack* Ben?"

"Yup, because he was told that Ben was a rat."

"A rat?"

"A stoolie, a songbird, a squealer."

"I see," she replied. "Why was it Matt's job to do the deed?"

"Because he was told to."

"By who?"

"Never mind."

"Alright, go on."

"After the deed was done, Matt found out that Ben wasn't a squealer at all. It was all a setup by a guy named, um..."

"Tom Cruise?" she quipped.

I laughed, then she smiled, revealing her huge Hollywood smile. "Okay, Tom Cruise. Cruise set up Ben and got Matt to fall for the con game hook, line, and sinker while offing Matt's best friend in the process."

"His best friend?"

"Since childhood."

"How horrible."

"Yes."

"Did Matt get to confront Cruise for what he did?"

"His friends did. It's all set. Cruise won't be playing anymore reindeer games."

Alex stood, hand-pressed the wrinkles from her

skirt and looked at her diplomas on the wall behind her—as if to draw guidance from them. I stood too and waited for the verdict.

"Nicky, I think..., I think I need to proceed very cautiously here. My job is not to judge. I do want to say that I'm very sorry for the loss of your friend's friend, and God knows that Matt needs extensive therapy to deal with the tremendous guilt he must be feeling. So, with that being said, I think we need to get right to work."

She extended her hand to me in a "done deal" kind of a way, so I accepted it. As her warm and smooth hand fit exquisitely in mine, I imagined drawing her amazing body into mine, then holding the goddess-like creature in my arms before gazing into her two teardrop-shaped and exotic-like eyes.

As she spoke, I continued my fantasy, out of control. I imagined my right hand, palm cupping her baby-soft face, while my thumb lovingly caressed her high cheekbones with four fingers, ever so lightly, holding the back of her delicate head which pressed gently upon her angelic hair that smelled like snow.

"Nicky, I think that's your cell phone ringing," Alex said, reaching for her appointment book on her desk behind her and breaking my fantasy. "You okay?"

The phone screen said Grace. I let it go to voicemail, ashamed that I did.

"I have a cancellation for tomorrow, if you want to come back that early. This way we can get started right away. I've never had anybody like you before, Nicky. It's going to be quite interesting."

"Likewise," I said. "See you tomorrow, Alex."

EIGHT

Most of my crew were waiting for me at Helen's Diner. I walked in, made the hand signal and they all got up and followed me to Anna's Restaurant instead. That threw off any plans of pre-planted bugs the Feds might have had. They hated when we did that. We headed to Anna's.

After the coffees were served, I spoke above everyone else. "Where's Brendon?" I asked.

"He's got a stomach virus thing," Brandon replied.

"This is the second meeting missed because of a stomach virus thing this month," I said. "Somebody said he was drinking heavy at Lucia's on Saturday night. He's casting sunlight on himself. You know how we feel about staying under the radar. Let your brother know that if he can't do this, we'll get someone to take his place, and he can watch from the Providence River. From underneath it."

"I... I will tell him, Skipper."

"Alright, let's get down to business. What do we know about Carmine's kid, Nicholas? Where is my loving godson?"

Bobby C took the lead. "We know the Feds have him under armed guard, 24/7. He's in one of the Quonset huts on the National Guard Base in Cranston. We're told that he wants complete freedom for his testimony. He's holding out until he gets it."

"What did he know about his old man's business?"

"Nothin," Iron Mike answered. "We think he was too young to remember Carmine's doings, but he's making the Feds think he knows things."

"But he says he saw you whack his old man, Skipper," Friday Night chimed in. "And he wants you to pay for that."

I exploded!! My hands were around Friday's neck in two seconds! I had him up and against the wall, with my nose pressed against his, seething! Seething!

"Who said I killed him? Who? Who said it? I didn't fuckin' do nothin' to Carmine, and if I ever hear anybody say anything like that again I'm gonna go postal on every one of you mother fuckers!"

By the time I let go of Friday's neck, he had ten perfect fingerprints on his chicken neck!

A quiet came over us and things settled down. Way down. Friday and I plopped down on our seats and breathed heavy through our noses for a few minutes until we didn't. He apologized profusely, so I eventually got back to business.

"Alright," I said. "Work hard on this one. I want you guys to call in all your favors and find a way to get to that kid. *Capische*?" They all understood what that meant.

During breakfast we talked about the sports gambling thing of ours, as well as our loan-sharking business. Friday's head still hung low. He's been too loyal for me to hold a grudge. Before I left, Bobby updated us on our earnings from state construction bids, then we were done. Just like that. Profits were good, so I instructed him to give Father Mario another envelope. Ten grand this time. My wife joined a committee to raise money for a new roof for the church, so I made sure I did my heavenly duty.

I headed out the door to a busy day ahead of me. My pickup was in sight right outside the window, so there was no need for my key drop and swoop.

I decided to visit Lucky at St. Mary's hospital.

That would give me a good excuse to visit with Alex. Did I just say Alex? I meant Jessie. Well, at least I'm not thinking about Star anymore. Oh shit! Grace! I forgot to call Grace back! I dialed right then, but there was no answer, so I just hung up without leaving a message.

The hospital was busy. People moving like little soldier ants, as if all on a serious mission. The receptionist gave me Lucky's room number which was on the fourth floor. I found it easy enough and knocked before entering. Lucky's wife was there and so was a prosthetic eye doctor, fitting him for a new eyeball. *Friggin' creepy*, I thought.

"Hi Nicky," the gambler said, somber, as if he'd just lost a big bet and was about to cry.

"Hello Lucky, is this your wife?"

"She's my sister. I live in her and her husband Vernon's basement–for the time being. Phyllis this is Nicky Mancusso, a guy I know. Say hello, Phyllis."

"A guy you know?" I said.

"Actually, yeah...sorry, you're right, Nicky. Phyllis, Nicky is the guy whose men found me after the truck hit me. I mean the car. I mean the hit and run accident."

"It's nice to meet you, Nicky."

"Same here, Phyllis. Lucky has told me so much about you."

"Really? Did the stunada (*stoonad* - meaning stupid, idiot) tell you that I hate his lying, good for nothin' guts, and I wish you'd of left his deadbeat, lazy ass out there in the street for some other sap to take in? This way the mooching would stop, and I'd have a chance for a real life! No more phone calls from thumb-breakers looking for Lucky! Jesus, I wouldn't know what to do with myself!"

I turned to the prosthetic guy to check out the eyeballs in his display tin.

"How you doing?" I said, as I watched him pluck a blue eyeball from the display. Prosthetic eye-guy raised his eyebrows but never said a word. "What's up with the blue ones, Lucky? Your eyes are brown?"

"Yeah, I know that Nicky, but this guy says he'll give me a deal if I take a blue one off his hands. He's got too many of them. I figure what the hell."

"See! My brother's a stunada!" Phyllis said. "One brown eye and one blue eye, he'll look like a freak show! But does he care? Noooo! What girl will marry him now? Fuckin' loser!"

"Okay, it was nice meeting you, Phyllis! I gotta go."

I then leaned over Lucky, pretending to kiss him goodbye but whispered in his ear instead. "Lucky, I bought your debt. The one from the New York guys. Don't miss a payment to us, or you'll be wishing we left you with those guys, having your head squished like a grape in a wine press. We dropped an envelope with their five-thousand in it before sending them a message not to fuck with us here in Rhode Island. You owe that to us now. You're welcome, by the way."

"Five-thousand? What five-thousand? Nicky, I owed them Ten large! You short changed them five grand!"

"Are you kidding me? How the frig do you owe them ten?"

"There was this sure thing tha..."

"Lucky! Are you serious! I should have let them squeeze your other..., never mind. I'm outa here."

I left. No goodbyes. Just left.

Still steamed, I pushed the elevator button marked C for cafeteria. *Those NYC guys will be back for sure,* I thought.

I was hoping that Jessie would be having her lunch at noon outside by the statues of the saints in the garden. I was right. There she was, sitting by herself on a marble bench next to the Virgin Mary. She had an extra sandwich sticking out of a paper bag, a telltale sign she was hoping I'd show up.

Her smile said it all. "Hi Nicky, hungry? Got time for a quick game of gin rummy?" Jessie was cute. Not Alex cute. Not Star cute. She was the kind of girl you take home to mom–cute. Like Grace.

"Nicky, I was just going over notes from my attorney for the start of the trial this week. I just wish he would plead guilty to assaulting me and all those other women, but he won't. Woody Woodrow Getz has no remorse and won't stop unless he's caught red handed. Look at my hands shake. I'm a nervous wreck having to relive this all over again."

"Is your father going to be in the courtroom for you, Jess? For support?"

"Yes, but I'm afraid my dad won't be able to contain himself and might jump over the courtroom seating to get to Getz when he sees him. His two-thousand-dollar suits along with his handpicked "dream team" legal staff will be just enough to drive my dad over the edge. I worry about him"

"It'll be okay, Jessie. Things will work out for you, I have faith. Look to your right, what do you see?"

"Um..., the Blessed Mother," she replied.

"Close your eyes and pray to her," I said. Tell her what you need. Tell her what you want, and if the prayer is possible, you will get it. Have faith in her, okay? My Grandma taught me that when I was a kid. Try it. I have to go."

"You have to leave?" She stood to kiss my face, positioned two fingers on the scar on my throat and held them there, lightly, before slowly lifting them to place the wrapped cellophane sandwich in my hand.

"Bye Jessie Jayne, my friend."

"Goodbye, Nicky, my friend. Thank you."

I finally made it to the Pink Pussycat. It was steady but not overly busy, especially with the just so-so looking daytime dancers on duty at that time.

Scammy was tending bar as usual. That guy worked day and night for the almighty dollar. I don't know what he did with his money, because he sure didn't spread it around. Every night when it was time to tip out the girls, that cheap bastard would try every which way to gyp them. I'm surprised he's made it this long.

I signaled to No Neck Nunzio that he, Bruno Luccetti and Antonio Santini needed to have a sit-down with me right away.

The Consigliere, Underboss and Boss were usually invited to a sit-down when available. But the Boss makes the final decision on the matter, period.

No Neck sensed the importance and urgency in my face, so he barged through the patrons and made his way to the way-back room in no time. Then returned just as fast with a head nod for me to follow. Of course, Scammy, that ficcanaso (pronounced *fica noz* - nosy, busybody) stretched his neck out like a giraffe standing on its tiptoes and followed my movements until I was out of sight.

No Neck and I walked past a high-stakes poker game in the back room before reaching the way-back office, an off-limits area with a penalty of unimaginable consequences to violators stupid enough to break the rules.

My underboss, *Bruno the wop*, met me at the door with a big grin and a giant cigar.

"Hello, Bruno," I said, before kissing and hugging him like he was family. Actually, he was family. My other family.

"Nicky, *come sta* (pronounced *co me sta* - How are you)? How's my favorite Caporegime?" (pronounced *capo rejeem*) *Captain, head of the regime or crew* (from the Roman Legion).

Bruno liked to speak Italian or at least mix it up a little. I could hold my own but only in slang and the Italian dialect. Proper Italian was like speaking proper English. It wasn't for me.

"Bene, sto bene Bruno, e tu?" I asked.

"I'm glad you're doing good, Nicky. I'm good too, grazie–thank you. Come in, come in!"

Antonio Santini looked lost behind his desk. Old age had taken over his body, shrinking him down to a fraction of what the man once was.

The boss stood and greeted me with wide-opened arms. His stogie dangled out the corner of his mouth, but he managed not to drop it. Years and years of practice, I guess.

"We know why you're here, Nicky," Boss Santini said, looking over at Bruno for acknowledgement, which he got with a nod. "We got a call from a little bird in New York that said the envelope was shy. Alright, they slipped and fell, that's understandable but shorting them on their take? Why? You made a deal and gave them your word to make them whole. That's not like you, Nicky. The New York family will not look favorably on that. Sit down, please. Have a cup of espresso." I nodded, no."

I sat, but Bruno and No Neck remained standing

behind me, which I didn't like. I didn't like that at all. I've seen guys clipped for far less.

I began to answer the boss, while keeping all my senses on the two behind me, and secretly acknowledging the .380 in my ankle holster.

"I didn't know the payoff was twice that amount and didn't stiff them intentionally. That's the truth."

Santini relit his crooked stogie cigar. Who knows how long ago it went out? A dense puff of smoke surrounded the old man in charge and yet he spoke through it anyway.

"Bruno will make a call today on your behalf. Nunzio will drive to their city and make good on your debt. The toothless wonders will probably still come at you with all they have, and that's something you are going to have to contend with. You sealed your fate when you made them eat their own teeth. That's something I can't help you with. Maybe you should have let them squeeze the puss from that pimple, Lucky. I hear he is a degenerate gambler anyway. Well, that was your call and you own it now. Good luck, Nicky and take care of your family. This is all I have to say."

That meant the sit-down was over. No more talks, no more discussion. Not another word.

Before leaving the club through the side door, I glanced back at the bar and noticed Ronnie T sitting at the end. He covertly raised his hand inches from his beer glass in a salute to me and my status. I always liked Ronnie, he was a good earner, and I wished he was in my crew rather than Jimmy the Weasel. I think he did too.

While going through the door, a woman blew in past me, stopping in her tracks as soon as I was recognized.

“Nicky! Nicky! It was Star. It was Star, standing in the doorway of the Pink Pussycat nightclub. I hadn’t seen her dressed like that since her sister Moon was found in her Beamer with an icepick stuck in her eye. It looked weird, surreal, and I couldn’t wrap my mind around it. Star looked good. Still sexy. I hadn’t seen her since the hospital visit. Still flawless. Still... *Oh my God! Grace! I forgot to call Grace back, again! Shit!*

“Hello Kid,” –still walking, letting her know I was in a hurry. “What are you doing here, Star?”

“I have a meeting with the house mom. I’m starting this weekend. Yup, I’m coming back to the Cat!”

I’m cursed. I’ve just got to be. “That’s great Star, honey. That’s great. I can’t talk now though. I’ll see you around, soon, okay?”

"Okay, I see you're in a hurry. I'll see you soon and will tell Nicki you said hi. You look great, Nicky. See you soon. Hey...Nicky?"

"Yeah?"

"I missed you."

"I missed you too, Star. Gotta go." *Yup, I'm cursed.*

Slowing down the approach to my pickup, I pretended to drop my keys on the pavement, reached down to retrieve them, and took an extra-long survey of the bottom of my undercarriage. The lift kit I had installed on the already high 4-wheel drive truck gave the Chevy four more inches of ground clearance, making it easier for someone to place a pipe bomb, but also made it easier for me to see it if they did. All seemed clear. After the attempted assassination on me by Carmine's kid, I took things more seriously and found myself reciting the Lord's Prayer as I turned the key in the ignition. By the time I was *lead us not into temptation,* I had my seatbelt buckled, the mirrors positioned, and the song I liked selected on the radio.

My cellphone rang. It was Grace. The sigh I let out seemed endless. "Hello?"

"Did you listen to my message, Nicholas? From hours ago?" *Oh boy, now it's Nicholas?*

"I did not, Grace, was it important?"

Crying into the phone in a garbled and desperate voice, she tried to answer. "Carla tried to commit suicide! I guess the thought of losing her son to the law, *and* her husband to a monster, was too much for her. She's in intensive care! I haven't left her room all day! Why didn't you call me, Nicky? Did you even think of me at all?"

"Yes! I did, Grace! I did! In fact, I was just talking to Star and..."

"You met Star!"

I even said to her, shit, I was supposed to call Grace! Hello? Grace? Are you there, Grace? Are you with me?"

"I was," Grace said, "but not anymore." *Click.*

NINE

I spent the night at the shop. The shower I installed when I was younger reminded me of the old days. When I was young, I had girls falling at my feet, sported a wad of cash in my pockets, and an ego that made me too big for my britches. When I almost lost Grace.

The extra clothes I had in my office were from those days too and were so far out of date it was laughable. The tassels on my shoes were almost as bad as the "members only" shirts on the pink hangers. What a *scumbari* I was. Still am (pronounced *shkoom barree* - embarrassment).

The next morning, I headed over to my therapy session in my Baywatch-era attire. *Just what I wanted to wear for Alex,* I thought.

She looked phenomenal as usual —and after eyeing my retro get-up, she wanted to get right to it.

"How does Matt Damon feel about what he did to Ben Affleck?" I waited before answering, scanning the room for hiding places for bugs and scrutinizing her game for holes in it. Meaning, I needed to feel comfortable that nothing could connect me with Matt —or Carmine with Ben.

Still uneasy, I found nothing that could incriminate me, so I still played along. Kind of like how O.J. did when he wrote the book, "If, I did it."

I answered her. "I hear he feels guilty, of course. How could he not?" My tone was a little cocky, so I walked it back a little. "Um, anyone in his position would have done the same thing though, right? Right?"

"I don't know, Nicky. Tell me more. You said Matt and Ben were friends. Were they close?"

"They would have died for each other."

"Then why the hatred? Why would Matt throw out a lifetime of friendship, but more importantly, why would he kill his best friend because someone told him to?"

"Because, at the time, he supposedly cooperated

with the law. There is nothing worse than a rat, and rats need to be exterminated."

We spoke for a while more, playing her little name game and running out the clock. Before I knew it, it was time to go.

"When would you like to make another appointment?"

"Let's do it soon please. I'd like to get these six sessions over with as soon as possible. I'm halfway through them, so we need to work fast to fix me and rid me of this guilt thing. Oh, before I forget, this is for you." I reached into my waistband and pulled out a tiny box wrapped in what looked like a piece of used, crinkled, party wrapping paper.

"Nicky, how nice! But I...I can't. I can't accept this though. I make it a policy to keep it professional. No gifts, but thank you."

"It's not what you think, Alex. Open it." I put it in her hand. "Trust me, open it." Blushing only complimented her chosen array of makeup.

"Okay, I'll make an exception, just this time." With finger and thumb, she methodically picked at the seam of the wrapping paper, displaying her high-end manicure job that matched her wardrobe, her Porsche, her lifestyle.

She peeled back the paper and revealed the tiny hinged box. That made her look up at me with disapproval.

"Open it, Alex."

Peaking under the lid, she started slow–then almost snapped the hinges right off! "My mom's locket! You found my mom's locket! How! How did you find my mom's stolen locket! Oh my God!"

Clutching the vintage necklace, she quickly brought it to her lips, then just as fast opened it to check for the picture inside.

Satisfied, Alex held it to her chest, as streams of tears ran down her cheeks, along with a tinge of mascara, but she didn't know. She quickly closed the distance and displayed the most excitable happiness!

Throwing both arms around me, she pulled herself into my body, tight. Really tight, with no sign of letting go.

My fantasy was coming true before my eyes. Now don't get me wrong, I didn't retrieve the hot locket because of hopes for that moment. I really didn't. Helping good people is what I do. I believe in helping the homeless, helping the helpless, it's just that when it comes to business, I don't give a shit about the clueless.

Just as I inhaled her heavenly fragrance, it was over. Exhaling it, she was already two steps back, so I held my breath to let it out slowly, savoring every last drop before it was gone. "Nicky, I don't know how to thank you!"

"Your reaction is thanks enough. You're welcome."

My phone vibrated a single time in my pocket, so I glanced at it quickly. It was from Friday Night. The text read, "Clark Kent." It used to be code for 'call me from a phone booth.' It was a leftover code from the old days. I know there aren't any phone booths available anymore, in fact we all laughed when the Superman movie first came out and Clark Kent rushed to a phone booth to change, only to discover an open-air payphone sitting atop a short aluminum pole. But for whatever reason we still used the code "Clark Kent."

"I have to go, Alex. Something important has come up."

"You've made me a very happy girl, Nicholas Mancusso. My mom too."

"I'm glad. Gotta go."

I rushed out the door and made it to my shop in less than five minutes. Stashed away in the bottom of one of the sawdust buckets and sealed in an extra-large, zip-lock bag were three throw-away cell phones.

Untraceable. I picked out the oldest-looking one. It was a flip phone. I dialed and waited.

"It's me, what's up."

"We got problems."

"Like what?"

"They got Bobby C."

A sigh. "Alright. Meet me at that place. The place that the short guy likes. The place with the kittens. Translation: Meet me at Roger Williams Park Zoo. Where the boss fed Johnny Moonlight to the lions.

"Right."

Before leaving my shop, I ran to the supply room and found the bag of Mr. Green Thumb's Organic Cow Manure. I threw a vinyl glove on and stuck my hand all the way in the bag. It took me just seconds to pull out a Tupperware container covered in bullshit. Tearing off the cover on the way out of my building, I lifted a well-preserved, nine-millimeter, cocked it, and stuck it in my pants, in the back, under my belt.

The Zoo was full of families. No cops or Feds to be seen.

After making my way through the turnstile, I spotted Brandon and Brendon Sacoccia at a picnic table by the pond, throwing grass clippings into the water where the ducks were swimming. The two cucuzzas (pronounced *googootz*, squash, idiots), weren't aware that the ducks were not even remotely interested, and it immediately pissed me off.

Iron Mike and Friday Night came walking in from the left and Tony "Jackpot" Canatta and Tommy "Gag" Gaglione trotted in right behind them, from probably parking their car in the rear.

"Sit down, everybody," I ordered, giving the Sacoccias the stink-eye as they did. "Do you call that staying under the radar? Doing stupid shit in public? Do ducks eat grass clippings, assholes? Friday, deduct one C note from each of their pays this week. If they get hungry enough let them eat grass clippings."

"Okay, Skipper."

"Now tell me what we know about Bobby C?"

"Tell him, Jackpot. Go ahead," Friday nudged his arm, noticeably shaken.

"Well, Skipper..., my mother's cousin Angelina lives above Ventitullo's Bakery on Federal Hill. Every morning, she likes to sit with her tea by her second story window and watch who comes and goes. She's a widow and it's kind of a pastime for her."

"Get to the point, Jackpot," Iron Mike interrupted, pissy.

"Sorry. Well, anyway. She said that Bobby Castratoro comes in every morning, at exactly the same time."

"Bad move," I chimed in. "Have you guys learned nothing? Continue, Jackpot."

"She said he doesn't stay long, just enough time to get his chocolate-topped cannoli and bread for the family."

"Jesus Christ! She even knows what kind of cannoli he eats? Alright, come on, come on, you guys are killing me. Finish the story!"

"So, today she watched him park his car across the street, enter the bakery, stay in there maybe ten minutes, and exit with a box of pastry and a loaf of Italian bread under his arm.

Only today she said he was met by a guy flashing a shiny badge. Like a cop! After a brief conversation the cop walked Bobby to his van which was parked right in front and acted like he was showing Bobby something inside the already-opened, side sliding door."

"But when Bobby looked in, two other guys came out of nowhere and pushed Bobby inside, hopping in and closing the door behind them. Cousin Angelina thought he got pinched and was thrown inside a black-colored, unmarked paddy wagon until later on when she told my mother that the cop who pushed Bobby in the van was as big as a house and not anywhere near in shape, like a cop.

Cousin Angelina's a little "*shaquad*," (empty-headed). That's when my mother called me, and I called Friday Night."

"Yeah, Jackpot called me right away, Friday Night said. "Bobby's car is still parked where he left it, I checked–and our guy on the inside told me that Bobby Castratoro was not brought to the Providence or State Police Departments today. Those New York guys have him, Skipper."

"I know. I know. Okay, let me think! Alright, Jackpot..., I want you and Tommy Gag to hit every business, tenement, anyone you can think of that might have a security camera pointed at the street in front of Ventitullo's bakery. Start with cousin Angelina. I want the license plate number of that van! It's got to have Rhode Island plates. Bobby would never have fell for that con if it had New York tags. If I'm right, they're working with someone in our own backyard, after all, a third guy was seen with Heckle and Fuckin' Jeckle–and I find that very interesting."

"Brandon and Brendon, I want you to split up.

Shadow each and every one of us. Watch us for tails. And I don't mean cops or feds. One of us may be next, so follow us to see if we are followed. Lay low. No feeding ducks, no stupid shit in public. Can you do that? Can you stay out of the spotlight?"

"Yes, sir," Brandon said.

"We can do that," Brendon followed.

"Those two guys, uh...that Mountain character and his side kick Crazy Carlo shouldn't be hard to spot if they're still in Providence."

"Friday and Iron Mike, I want you guys to hit the streets in Providence. Contact every snitch, every bookie, every hooker, and nun. Somebody, somewhere, knows something. Find out what and don't come back until you do."

"I'm heading to the club. Although I don't think it matters, I need to find out when the rest of Lucky's buyout payment was sent to New York and if and when it was received. Let's keep in touch. Now go, Bobby doesn't have much time."

TEN

In the mad rush to get to the club, I forgot to do the "swoop" before getting into my truck, and I was mad at myself for that. *It's more important than ever, don't forget it again.*

I noticed that I had three missed calls. The first was from Star, the second was from Alex, and the third was from Grace.

"Un-fuckin' real," I said out loud to myself. "The only one missing is Jessie Jayne."

"There it is!" I said, louder to myself than before. The phone rang, buzzed, vibrated, and lit up all at the same time! It read, "Jessie Jayne!" *Now I know I'm cursed.*

Ignoring Jessie's call, I pulled into the Pink Pussycat and into my usual spot. Then put it in reverse, backed out, and pulled into a different spot right in front of the door.

"Meathead," the bouncer was at the front door, so I handed him two fins and told him to watch my truck extra carefully.

The club was hoppin'. Dancers were on stage two at a time, so that meant there were many. Scammy had a club soda already poured for me, as I walked by the bar. No time for a signal to No Neck this time for an invitation. I walked right into the back room, around the occupied card tables, and straight back to the way-back office where the boss resided. You'd of thought I was barging into the oval office in the Whitehouse!

Mon-edge-a-son-don-dawn! (spelled-mannaggia San Antonio!) God damned Saint Anthony! Guys came out of the woodwork! And just think, I'm a Captain! A Capo! Imagine if a civilian tried to get back there?

After Santini called the dogs off and let me in his office, I kissed both his cheeks, sat right down, and plead my case in the smoke-filled, poorly-lit, throw-back of an office.

"Listen, Nicky. You're a good boy. But I told you that after I squared away the other half of Lucky's debt with New York, I could do no more." I glanced up and silently paid my respects to the Virgin Mary and Frank Sinatra. Still amazed at how 'old blue eyes' had top billing on the wall over the Mother of God.

"Antonio, can you please tell me if and when you sent that payment to New York? I'm thinking that if they didn't get it yet, then maybe that's what this is all about."

"Naw. They got the payment. I didn't want to wait, so I had my *gumbada* from Queens take a cab over and pay them on our behalf."

"Is our talk secure here, Antonio?"

"Si, go ahead. I just had this office swept yesterday. There are no bugs."

"Then I will ask. Who did your *gumbada* pay then?"

"I had him pay Domenic."

"He paid Domenic Romano? The boss himself?"

"Of course I had him pay the boss himself. Domenic said he knew nothing about things but took the money anyway, naturally. He said he would check into it."

Santini sat back in his dilapidated chair, pushed the spilled ashes from his desk into his hand, and ground them into his palm. "He knew," Santini continued. "He knew all about it. Not that he's a *cazzate* *(*bull-shitter*)*. And I'm not saying he is. I'm just saying he knew. Bosses always know. *Io muri hanno orecchi (*walls have ears*). Capische*, Nicola?"

"*Si, capische*, I understand. Then tell me, Antonio. What do the walls say about Bobby Castratoro, one of my most valued and loyal soldiers?"

"They tell me that you are in danger. You can either strike first or strike last. *Se scegli di tenere il lupo per le orecchie, a di non fare niente e di fare certe cose sono altrettanto rischiose.* If you choose to hold the wolf by the ears, doing nothing and doing something are equally risky."

"Then you give me permission to strike?"

"Why do you ask for my permission now? Before, you made someone from another family bite down on a guardrail! Why did you not ask permission then? You know the rules, Nicola. Within our territories you have a wide range of latitude– except, naturally that is, with "friends of ours." But away from our territory, especially with other families, you have none. You risked starting a war, and now you must lie in your own bed. Now go."

Antonio Santini slowly stood, reached forward to kiss my cheeks and watched as I nodded that I understood the penalty. As I opened the door to exit, he cleared his throat loudly as if to speak.

"Nicola!" I stopped. "Remember, your crew is my crew. Be loyal to them and they will do the same. Protect them and they will do the same. The saying goes, "The only people I owe my loyalty to are those who never made me question theirs."

"I'll remember, Antonio."

"One more thing, Nicola."

"Yes, Antonio."

"Eve had the desire for the sweet fruit. Adam did not. Eve was weak. I suggest you start your search where Bobby was most vulnerable. His weakness may hold the key."

"Thank you, Antonio. I will do that." I paused in deep thought for about three seconds. "I will certainly do that."

Running through the hodgepodge of poker tables and mismatched stools and chairs, I spotted No Neck at the door. By now everyone knew what was going on, and the look on Nunzio's face spelled empathy, which was good because I could use him.

"Come with me, Nunzio if you want to help." He was game.

We marched past Scammy and blew right out the door. At the last second, something told me to look back at the stage—and I did. Yeah, the girl on the stripper pole, it was Star. The door swung closed.

No Neck was used to me dropping my keys before getting into my pickup, so it was no big deal to him. He was probably glad I did. We hopped in just as the club's exterior lights came on.

As I flew out of the parking lot, I looked up at them in thought. *Where did this day go?*

My cellphone rang, again. *Butterflies, always those damn butterflies in my stomach every time I think of Grace. God damn it! Is it worth it?*

It was Jackpot calling.

"Hello?"

"Skipper."

"Yeah. What did you find out?"

"The deli across from the bakery has a security system pointed at the street. They let us view it but it's very grainy. Too grainy to make out the number plates on any vehicles, just colors. One thing's for sure though, you were right. They were not New York plates on that van. They were Rhode Island's. They had help here, Skipper."

"Yeah, I know. Meet up with the rest of the crew and wait for my call."

"Will do, Skipper."

"Where are we going, Nicky?" No Neck asked.

"To The Hill. What time is it? Never mind, we'll be there in a minute." And we were. My truck screeched to a stop in front of Ventitullo's bakery on Federal Hill. They were closed. Their lights were still on in the back though, because the good bakers bake all night long.

No Neck pounded on the door, and I had to tell him to cool it. I thought his fist was going to go right through the door. While we waited for the shuffling feet sound to unlock the chain and lock, I wondered who would kick whose ass. No Neck Nunzio Sabatoni, Iron Mike Tissoni, or that toothless scumbag, The Mountain.

I was thinking that without teeth, Mountain must be one ugly son of a bitch by now. Suddenly, the bakery door swung open and old man Ventitullo appeared in the doorway. I figured he had to be in his early nineties by then.

"Mr. Vent, it's me, Nicky Mancusso." After staring and calculating things for a second, Mr. Vent spoke with unexpected, youthful energy.

"Nicky! Madonna mia! Come in! You eat? I got some nice spinach pies, just came out of the oven. Come on, sit down. Mangia!"

"We can't Mr. Vent, you remember Nunzio, huh?"

"*Bella chicoria*!" (beautiful dandelion-like greens). "Of course, I remember little Nunzio! You see! You see him now? He used to run by the baker shop, this skinny little kid, and I would make him stop and come in for calzones and..."

"Mr. Vent, please. We are in a hurry. I have to ask you a question, please. Bobby Castratoro, you know, Bobby C? Has anybody come in here asking about him in the past few days? Please, try to remember. It's important."

"Wait a minute. Let me think. Not that I remember. I'm sorry Nicky, I would remember if a stranger asked me anything about Bobby. You know I keep my nose clean and my mouth shut, don't you?"

"I know you do. You've been good to the family for years. We don't forget it. You would not forget a stranger, yes, but what about someone you know. Has his name come up from anybody you know?"

"Bobby C? Um... no, nobody. Nobody I can think of. Oh, just Mrs. uh... what's her name. My daughter calls her the Pappagallo (parrot), because she never stops talking! She buys only the day-old pizza chips. *Mannaggia Madonna mia*, they're only twenty cents more, fresh! Ah...what's her name?"

"What did she ask you about Bobby C, Mr. Ventitullo? Please remember."

"Same old stuff. She wants to know everything about everybody's business, and she nags her poor husband to death. I think she wanted to know if he still picks up his pastries every morning. She said something about seeing him every morning at eight but hadn't in a while. I assured her that he's still like clockwork and here every day at eight. That's all."

"Think hard, Mr. Vent. What's her name?"

"I wish I could..., wait, it's, it's..., Phyllis! Phyllis Luckett! The Irishman's sister! Lucky Luckett's sister, Phyllis! Alright? You boys wanna eat now?"

After leaving two C notes on the pastry counter, we didn't waste one minute getting over to Lucky's. No Neck called Friday and Mikey, who called Brandon and Brendon, who called Jackpot and Tommy Gaglione.

They met us in front of Lucky's sister's house, parking away from the streetlights and arriving all at about the same time.

Because I knew my lead guys so well, I told No Neck to stay behind and watch the street. Friday Night and Iron Mike had my flanks, so I went right up the front walk and rapped on the door. The other guys watched the garage and the back.

From inside the house, that damn dog started barking from the minute we pulled up, nonstop, without taking a dog's breath! It sounded like those Chihuahua-type, ankle-biter friggin' things!

Brandon gave a short whistle between barks and pointed through the window of the garage. He nodded his head continuously, while mimicking the turning motion of a steering wheel. I mouthed the words, "black van?" He continued nodding his head.

"Who's out there?" a male voice demanded, over the nerve-racking and never-ending yelp of that damn dog. Then we heard Phyllis's screechy squawk competing with them both. Phyllis won, hands down.

Lucky's sister from hell screamed the mother of all screams, and I thought my ears would start bleeding right then and there!

"Vernon, you piece of shit! Put the damn muzzle on that fuckin'dog!" Phillis ordered.

"I'm getting it, I'm getting it! You get the door!"

We didn't wait. Iron Mike predicted our next

move and was suddenly standing right next to me. One look told him what I wanted and when. He immediately opened the screen door, puffed up his upper body with a deep breath and with his right shoulder, he hit that front door so hard I thought the whole frame would come down. Some of it did and landed on Vernon, knocking him across the room and what looked like out cold!

Over Phyllis's constant and blood curdling shriek, we all barged in, single file, with no regard for property or pets. Bobby C was our only concern, so when Brandon drop-kicked that annoying mutt halfway into two rooms over—and when Brendon pried Precious's rhinestone-studded muzzle from Vernon's closed fingers and headed toward Phyllis, I didn't give a shit or even think twice.

I joined Iron Mike in searching the house, room by room, then, instructed Jackpot and Tommy to search the basement where Lucky resided, but they came up fairly quickly—empty handed.

Regrouping in the living room was a huge letdown, especially without finding our Bobby, either dead or alive. But the sight of seeing the Sacoccia brothers sitting on top of Phyllis— all three of them on her Italian-American, traditional, plastic-covered couch, with poochie's muzzle strapped to Phyllis's face like a "Fifty Shades" kind of thing, well, any other time I would have peed my pants right there and then.

"Friday, go get Fluffy. If he's alive," I said. "That drop-kick that Brandon hit him with must have sent him into next Tuesday, but check!

"I got him right here, Skipper," he answered, holding the mutt by the scruff of his neck.

"Okay, Mikey get a glass of cold water and hit Vernon's face with it. And you two guys, get off of Phyllis. You can take that muzzle off her pretty face too. If she makes one peep, Friday? You snap Toto's neck."

Phyllis slowly and cautiously raised her left hand, hair disheveled and eyeballs quite big.

"Yes, Phyllis?"

"His name is Lovey, not Fluffy."

"I'm so sorry, Phyllis. Fright Night?"

"Yes, Skipper?"

"If Phyllis makes one peep? Snap Lovey's neck." Laughter erupted from my crew, quietly though. We were still worried about Bobby. "Mikey picked up Vernon and put him on the couch next to his wife. Brandon, I'm going to ask this happy couple some questions. If they even pause on a question that I ask, if for even a second, each time they do, you'll rip something off of Lovey. "You know, like an ear or a paw or something. Start with his cute little tail, or balls if he has them. After that, you can pick."

I turned to Brandon and the rest of my crew and winked. Then, for good measure, looked directly at Brandon and winked again. I wanted to know he saw me and remembered our rules. We don't hurt people that are outside of our world, and I hoped that Brandon knew that that meant innocent animals too. But Vernon and Phyllis didn't know that. That was my ace in the hole.

"Phyllis?" Her eyes, still huge.

"Ye..., yes? Please don't hurt my dog."

"It's all up to you, Phyllis. Now tell me. Do you know Bobby Castratoro?"

"Personally? I don't," she answered. I turned to Brandon, who still had the dog by its scruff. "Wait! I didn't mean it that way," she said. "I'm not trying to be funny! I..., I know who he is!"

"Who kidnapped him, Phyllis?" By now she was broken. Tears streamed down her cheeks and now smaller, her physique shrunk down into her plastic covered couch. She looked to Vernon, swallowed, and then spoke.

"Two New York guys did it. Bookies, loan sharks, whatever, I don't know. And, and they made Vernon help them. They used our van and with Vernon's help they picked Bobby C up in front of Venitulli's Bakery. They made Vernon drive the van and made me find out his routine. I told them his daily schedule and that made it easy." She looked downward.

"Why, Phyllis? Why did you do it?"

"Because! You try living this life with my loser brother and this weak excuse for a husband!"

"Hey!" said Vernon.

Phillis continued. "We met them last month when they did some dealings with Lucky. He wasn't home one day, so I gave them each a glass of homemade wine. Father Iannotti makes it on the hide and being half Irish and half Italian, I appreciate a good glass of homemade wine and the holy man sure knows how to do that.

Then they stopped by the other day and told us they knew who did the hit and run thing on Lucky. Bobby Castratoro! He did it! They said that he owed them money too, and they wanted to talk to him. Not hurt him, just break his legs. And, if we helped, they'd give us twenty-thousand dollars! Twenty-thousand!"

"We'd finally be able to move down to Florida, get

out of this cold, and away from my loser brother! The homes down there are half of what they are here. I could get a small job soldering jewelry and Vernon could sit on his ass down there instead of up here!

Look at him! Vernon doesn't have the balls even now to say a damn thing! Wanna see his balls? Look in my purse! That's where I carry them!"

"Did they pay you the twenty-k?"

"Not yet." Looking down again, – "The money's not coming, is it?"

"Where did they take Bobby, Phyllis?"

"I don't know, Nicky. I really don't!" Vernon shook his head just as she did.

"Brandon, put the dog down."

It peeled out on the overly-waxed floor and jumped up onto Phyllis, burying its head in her lap.

Reaching into my pocket, I pulled out a thick bank roll. Dropping the entire wad on the coffee table, I wanted it to cover the cost of the door and frame.

"Let's go guys." I didn't thank either one. It just wasn't in me.

We regrouped at Helen's Diner. Dolores Belaruse with the nice caboose was on duty and stared down Friday Night as soon as we came through the door.

She gave a little smirk as she turned to cut a piece of pie for someone, and I didn't know if that was good or bad.

The seven of us filled the diner's only round table. No one said a word. I sat in silence before erupting in anger! "*Ah Vaffangule!*" I hollered, fist punching the tabletop and lifting the salt, pepper, and sugar containers two inches off the table. "Where the hell is he!?"

Friday lifted his head high above the rest. I thought he was looking for Dolores or her caboose, but that wasn't the case. He was on to something.

"Guys," Friday said, still looking up above the rest of us, deep in thought. "Guys, what did that fat chooch say? Mountain or whatever his dumb fuckin' name is? He said something to Bobby, when Bobby had his nine-millimeter pushed against Shrek's temple."

A few of the guys gave a short chuckle. "A threat," Friday Night continued. "It was a threat, did you hear it, Skipper?"

"Yeah, I did, you're right. I did hear that. He said he was going to come back for each of us one by one. Then Bobby called Mountain something like "ass-boil," because of those bumps on his face,"—more laughter. "But I can't remember what else."

"I remember," Iron Mike interjected, "He called Bobby C something weird..., goofy. What was it? Wait...um..., I know, he called him, uh..., buckwheats. Yeah, that's what he called Bobby when Bobby had his gun barrel all up in that giant's nose. Buckwheats, whatever the hell that is."

Brandon spoke up from out of the blue. "Buckwheats? I know what that means." He turned and spoke quietly to his brother Brendon. "You know what that is don't you, Brendon? Buckwheats, from that Christopher Walken movie. Remember? I think it's a Sicilian thing, but that movie made it famous. Uh, 'things you do when you're dead,' or some fuckin' movie name like that."

"Oh yeah," Brendon answered, in an even quieter voice. "That was a good movie."

I chimed in, annoyed, wondering what would possess a mother to name her kids Brandon and Brendon. *She must have been a real beaut,'* I thought. "Do you two Siskel and Eberts want to share it with the rest of us? Brandon, let's hear it! Come on, time's going by!"

Brandon leaned forward to explain while we all leaned forward to listen.

"Well, from what I know it's like this. Buckwheats is one of the most painful ways to die."

"Why?" I asked, fast.

"Because you linger. It's a slow and agonizing death, Brandon answered. It's basically torture."

"How? Speak up!"

"Okay, Skipper, you take a 22-caliber gun, because it has the smallest bullet with the smallest amount of gunpowder. You can load it into either a rifle or a pistol, your choice. Then, you place the barrel of the gun up the guy's ass–and fire just one shot."

"The small bullet very rarely exits the body and that's what causes all the damage. It doesn't kill you right away! It's kind of like getting gut-shot only from the inside instead. The victim suffers in agony as he bleeds internally, sometimes for days. If he does manage to hang on, all the torn bowels begin to stink with infection, and the poor bastard rots from the inside out. One bowel infects the next bowel and so on. It's brutal. That's what buckwheats means, shooting someone up the ass and hoping they rot and stink. Sometimes the wounded can stay alive for days, if not weeks."

The room was silent. All you could hear were

motor sounds coming from the compressors in the Coke cooler and ice maker behind the lunch counter.

I looked over at Friday Night. He, being the closest to Bobby, would be the one to lose it. Lose it and go after those guys with all he had.

Iron Mike must have sensed it too and reached for the back of Friday's neck to offer a three or four second massage. It remained quiet, still.

The waitress took our order, but no one ordered any food, just beverages.

"Listen," I said, softly. "We need to keep cool. We need to keep cool and outsmart these guys. They're animals, they've already demonstrated that by what they did to Lucky. We can outsmart them and bring Bobby home, now think. Brandon?"

"Yes, Skipper."

"What else can you tell me about this movie you saw? Obviously, that's where Mountain got the idea. In that story, what did they do with the victim after they kept him alive? Was he tied up? Was he left in the woods? What?"

"I really don't remember. Do you Brendon?"

"Wait." The waitress placed coffee and soft drinks on the table–then left. "Okay, go ahead."

"I don't remember where they left him, Skip, I

just remember the guy laying in unbearable agony. In a fetal position, shivering from shock, or a fever, infection, or all of it."

"Yeah, I remember that part too," Brandon answered. "But where did they end up finding him? I don't know, I was just a kid when that movie came out." In deep thought, Brandon picked and peeled the paper label from his Cherry Coke bottle.

"Wait, was it a dumpster, Brendon? After they shot him up the ass in the movie, did they leave the guy in a dumpster? Isn't that where they found him?"

"Yes! You're right, that's it! Skipper, we need to check the dumpsters in Providence tonight! Before the garbage man empties them tomorrow. Tomorrow's trash day in the city!"

"No need," I replied. "There is just one dumpster that we need to check. The one in our backyard, the one that would make the biggest statement and really hit home. The one at the Pink Pussycat! Let's go!"

No Neck threw a C Note on the table and watched me drop my keys before getting into my truck. The four-car caravan was on the road in less than three minutes, blowing traffic lights, stop signs and crosswalks.

"I gotta tell ya, Nicky. I don't relish anyone sticking a gun barrel up *my* ass."

"You're not on the hit list, Nunzio. You weren't there that night. It's just me, Friday, Iron Mike, and the Sacoccia Brothers. Tommy Gag and Jackpot are under the radar which is in our favor. Let's use that. Hold on, I'm gonna beat this light." I floored it and just made it, praying there weren't any cops eyeing us.

With our high beams clicked on, we barreled into the club's parking lot and surrounded the dumpster in the dark corner of the lot. Way in the back.

Of course, the first thing I thought of was the night I hopped into Star's Beamer, was immediately distracted by her beauty, and then noticed the six-inch knife blade sticking out of her, well, actually, out of poor Moon's eye socket.

There we sat. Bright lights beaming down against a filthy garbage dumpster, praying that our good friend was laying inside and praying that he was not.

The first dome to light up was Friday's, then mine. As I jumped from my pickup, a familiar putrid smell engulfed my airways. I recalled siting by that rusty dumpster years ago, the night I broke into the club which ultimately exposed my ex-Capo

Johnny Munaletto, aka Johnny Moonlight and that freak detective, Lieutenant Howie Bergle. Moonlight ultimately got fed to the lions that night, and Bergle fertilized the Boss's tomato plants. Santini has Moonlight's coglionis (pronounced *cool e owns* - balls) proudly displayed in his office, under his beloved picture of Frank Sinatra and beside a picture of the Virgin Mary.

"I have a Maglite, Skipper," Jackpot yelled from the rear, pulling in directly behind me.

"Bring it up here! Tommy! You stay back and observe the whole scene. Make sure no one else is observing us, get it?"

"Got it!"

"Friday Night, open the lid. Careful, it's heavy, don't slam it." I endured that nauseating aroma years ago because I had to–this time I did because I wanted to.

The lid *was* heavy and it took both of Friday's hands to open it and let it land gently against the side of the dumpster. By the time he did, the whole crew was surrounding the opened top, careful not to touch the sides of the filthy, germ-ridden container.

"Jackpot, shine the light inside, hurry up!"

The Maglite was super powerful. Its beam hit

my eyes accidentally when he positioned himself between Friday and Mike, blinding me for a second until I blinked it away.

Being just half full, we had no choice but to grab onto the side rails and stand on our toes to see all the way to the deep bottom.

Arranged haphazardly before us, were torn and broken trash bags. They spilled out bathroom trash items, like soiled toilet paper with lipstick and skid marks, cigar and cigarette butts, along with mounds of wet ashes. Just all the things you knew you'd find in a dumpster.

Loosely spewed about everywhere, were unidentified food items that looked rotted, like decaying roadkill, that leaked disgusting fluids that were once solids.

Jackpot gagged with watery eyes, still attempting to point the beam from the Maglite inside the germ–ridden cesspool.

As his light beam continued to scan, it shined on the inside of the dumpster walls and revealed the drippings of what looked like milk, egg yolks, and vomit from the rest room floors after a Saturday night drinking party.

Suddenly, something stopped the light beam on a curious and suspicious target!

And, low and behold, laying close to the bottom of the dumpster in a fetal position, shivering, whimpering and unrecognizable, was our beloved, Bobby C, Bobby Castratoro.

ELEVEN

Friday Night's wail could have woken the dead throughout the Pink Pussycat's parking lot. It broke through the night's silence and shook me to the core.

"No!" Friday screamed. "Get him out of there! Get him out! Skipper!" I very rarely saw a grown man cry!

When Jackpot steadied his bright light on Bobby's fetal body, that's when we saw the first maggot scurry across my crew member's pale face. His eyes were open but he didn't blink.

Friday pleaded again. "Get him the fuck out of there, please!"

He then began going over the top and into the dumpster, head-first!

"Guys, guys! Grab him! You can't do it that way!" I screamed. "Friday, wait! Mikey, get Bobby outta there. Friday Night, step back! Do you want to fall and land on him! Everyone calm the fuck down."

Tommy and No Neck pulled Friday back and held onto him tight, keeping him out of the way.

"Breathe!" I said. "Everyone calm down and breathe. This is our friend. We need to do this right; that's a friggin' order!" Everyone de-escalated and obeyed. Cosa Nostra style.

"Alright, now, Brandon and Brendon are thin. You two guys go in gently and bring him up for the rest of us to grab onto. Once in, lift him up and over the side. The rest of us will catch our friend and gently lay him down. *Capische*? Does everyone understand?" They all nodded in silence. Everyone except Friday, he was in another world, thinking of his good friend at the bottom of that hell hole.

"Okay, let's go. Guys, help them into this thing."

The Sacoccia brothers didn't hesitate. No one smelled the putrid smell or were repulsed by the maggots anymore. We all just went right to work.

Along with a mess of food-blotted napkins and tissues stuck to Bobby's shirt, globs of who knows what was stuck to his bloody pants.

They kneeled down on the garbage and raised Bobby up, high enough for countless hands and arms to carry him up and over the side of the dumpster and land gently into Iron Mike's awaiting arms.

Friday leaned in and listened for signs of breathing but pulled away with a look of disappointment on his shattered face.

Suddenly, Friday startled us all, as if we needed any more friggin' surprised outbursts! "He blinked! I saw him blink! I swear to the Virgin Mary! There it is again, look!"

"He's right," Jackpot said, shining the light in Bobby's eyes and getting a small reaction.

"Don't get too excited, the fact that he's still alive could be a bad thing," No Neck said, out of sight from the rear and in the dark. I knew what he meant and he was right. There was blood everywhere, especially on his pants above his butt.

Just then, Bobby's body began to convulse! At timed intervals, it looked like he was having contractions! Friday kept talking to him and I was glad.

I delivered a soft-spoken order. "Let's put him in the back of your car, Friday. Mikey, carry him there, hurry! We will clear the way to St. Mary's emergency room for you. Let's go!"

Ignoring every red light and stop sign, I sped through the streets of Providence, like I was fleeing from trouble! As a kid, I was very good at that! I hit speed dial when a female voice answered.

"Jessie! It's me, Nicky! Are you on your shift? Are you at the hospital? Okay, I'm bringing someone in! I'll be there in three minutes! Will you have a stretcher waiting for us at the front door? Okay, listen! He's got a gunshot wound to the rectum. Yes, rectum. Jessie, what should we say? How do we say this happened? We say he was cleaning the gun? Are you kidding me, Jessie? I believe you that it happens all the time but in the rectum? Alight, alright! That's what happened then. Okay, we are pulling up to the door now! Do you see us?"

No Neck and I pulled up ahead and let Friday and Mikey park in front of the automatic doors. His car was quickly surrounded by doctors, nurses, orderlies, and police. And that was our cue, the police. We texted Friday as to what Jessie told us to say happened, and we pulled away, signaling Jackpot and Brandon to follow. As we drove off, I said The Lord's Prayer, forgot a few of the words, made up my own and headed for home.

"Don't forget, I have to get my car at the club," No Neck said, trying to wipe blood off of his shoes with spit and just his fingers.

After dropping him off, I sat back and took my time going home. I needed to decompress. B101, – that was the radio station of choice. The Kinks were playing Lola, my adrenaline was fading, we found a lost member of my crew, – and still! Still! I couldn't stop thinking of Carmine and what I did to him!

The house was completely dark. Grace didn't even leave a nightlight on for me. I guess I deserved it. She's put up with a lot from me and "The life." That's what we called it. "The life." We never say the "M" word.

Tiptoeing up the stairs to the bedroom, I remembered to avoid every creek and squeak on the stairs that would rat me out with no mercy. And, I was amazed on how well I still knew them. Leftover from my bigshot days, I guessed. It all scared me.

Am I going back to those womanizing days? I wonder which one will get me in trouble. I need to be strong. Up I went up the stairs, stepping lightly all the way.

Each time I stepped, I spoke in my mind.

This one's for Grace. There was silence.

Up I went.

This one is for Alex... no squeak.

I climbed another.

This one is for Star... not a peep.

Up another.

This one is for Jessie Jayne... Squeeeaak!

"Nicky, is that you?" Grace hollered. I could sense the concern in her voice.

"It's me, Grace." We haven't spoken in what seemed like forever.

"What time is it?" she asked.

"I have no idea."

That's all I got from her that night. She just rolled over and pretended to go to sleep.

The next morning came quickly. A text message was waiting for me on my phone. I'd heard the ding thirty minutes prior but just couldn't get up yet. I was exhausted, physically and mentally. And the long reach for the phone proved it was more physical.

When the light lit up my home screen, the name Star stood out like a sore thumb. The attachment that was clipped to her message was too small to view. Curious, I clicked that first. There she was, gone was her 'pulled below the ears,' Red Sox baseball cap, torn jeans, and flats. Back was her china doll hair-bob, exposed belly button ring, and stiletto heels, laced all the way up to her silky-smooth calves.

"Good morning, Nicky!" That's all it read. I sat for a second– thinking.

"Good morning, Star," I typed back, with one eye looking for the send button and the other on the bedroom door looking out for Grace. Without thinking about it I searched for the volume button to lower the sound. *Too late!* What should have been its usual "ding," sounded like the tremendous "gong!" you'd get before two Kung Fu opponents squared off in a Bruce Lee movie. It scared the living shit out of me!

To make matters worse, Grace entered the room with a laundry basket full of my folded clothes, still not talking to me. "Gong!" again it dinged in my phone and gonged in my mind. *Mannaggia, Madonna mia!* I lowered the volume.

Only when Grace placed the basket in front of my bureau, was I was able to steal a peek at the text message. This time, it wasn't from Star at all. It was from Friday Night.

Partly in code, it read:

"My daughter's kitty went under the knife last night for six hours due to that car accident. Poor little thing is in critical condition. Will know more today. Your friend who sits with the saints wants you to call her." Translation, Bobby C was operated on and Jessie Jayne wants me to call her.

I responded with "TY" and hopped in the shower for my appointment with Alex and then on to my usual business. I never did send that 'good morning' response back to Star and was glad I didn't.

The reserved parking space was occupied by a lipstick-red Porsche 911. Doctor Alexandria Elizabeth Pearlmutter sounded like such a stuffy name. Too stuffy for a lipstick-red, anything. I had to park in my usual loading zone, no parking spot on the street.

After the usual ceremonies from the front desk to the waiting room, I finally made it to Alex's office. In the past, each time she entered the room I was blown away and that day was no exception. A dress was worn instead of a skirt. Stunning. She just oozed sex appeal.

"Hello Nicky, I can't wait to tell you about my mother's reaction when I gave that locket back to her, thanks to you. I can't thank you enough! How are you today?"

"Oh, you're welcome, but I've been better." She began to make herself comfortable which made me uncomfortable.

Alex's dress was tighter than it should have been, and she started that continuous leg crossing thing again. Of course I peeked, briefly. Very briefly.

"What's the matter?" she asked. "Fall in love with your therapist yet?"

"What? No! Why would you..."

"Calm down, Nicky! It's just a joke! Haven't you ever heard that one before?"

"No."

She giggled a high-pitched giggle. "I'm sorry! That's an old one. They used to say, that in at least one point in a therapist slash patient relationship, the patient always falls in love with his or her therapist. I didn't mean to embarrass you, Nicky. I'm sorry."

"*Naw*, it's fine! Why would I be embarrassed?"

"Okay, let's start over. How was your day yesterday?"

"Not great."

"Please, tell me. What happened?"

"I can't."

"Oh, come on, nothing surprises me anymore. I've heard it all."

"Not this one you haven't."

"Want to bet lunch? I haven't eaten yet today," she said with confidence.

I could never refuse a bet, one of my vices left over from the old days, I guess. So, I reached for my keys and inspected my little surveillance detector on my keychain. It looked intact and activated. No bugs.

"You're on," I said–smirking like I did as a boy. I never lost that smirk.

"Okay, give me what you've got," she said.

If looks could kill, I thought.

"Are you sure?"

"I'm sure, nothing surprises me, give it to me," she said, switching her leg cross again.

Crossing my arms with a look of nonchalant, I told myself to be strong and began.

"Well Alex, unbeknownst to me, a guy I had been shylocking with took on another note from a couple of crumb bums from out of state, who didn't give the guy three minutes past his due date to make good on his payment, when they put his head in a vice and squeezed down so hard that it popped one of his eye balls out."

"So, me and my guys bought the loan, paid them off, sent them packing back to New York, had them bite down on a guardrail on Route 95, while my guy kicked the back of their heads so hard, their teeth were delivered to me later in a zip-loc bag."

"But the loan was for more than we thought, so, not only did we give each of those two guys the nicknames Gum and Gummer, we mistakenly gypped their family out of their due."

"So, in return, they put six of us on a hit list, grabbed one of my guys, beat him within an inch of his life, and then shot him up the ass before dropping him into a dumpster to suffer a long and agonizing death, alone and covered in maggots and swill. Ever hear that one before?"

Dead silence. One of her eyebrows was locked in a semi-vertical position while the other one pointed almost straight down. Her mouth tried to form a smile but something kept pushing it back to a serious expression. She didn't know exactly what to do.

"Alex, are you still with me?"

She thought for a moment before answering. "You win, Nicky Mancusso. Come on, I'll drive. I'm hungry anyway."

I didn't know which was worse, the death-defying drive in that little 911 or keeping my eyes everywhere else except on Alex. Every time her left heal pushed down on the clutch, the slit in her skirt opened wider, revealing a smooth, tanned thigh and reminding me of the night I sat next to lifeless Moon in Star's BMW.

Whiplash came to mind, while we swerved into the tiny parking lot at the eatery. It was like the car was on autopilot, as we came to an abrupt stop.

Acting like it was no big deal, I wobbly exited the vehicle and in we went.

The first thing she did was order a glass of white wine. I ordered seltzer water. Small talk was all hers and I just let her go.

As she bit into her bacon, lettuce, and tomato cheeseburger, I watched, listened, and learned. Like the inside of a gun barrel, I studied all the "lands and grooves" of her face. Every high and every low. She was captivating. Even the chards of lettuce caught between her teeth were erotic.

This was a bad idea, I thought.

"Nicky, I hope I haven't bored you at all with the story of my mom and her locket," she asked, leaning forward and forcing me to try a bite of her sandwich. *If she only knew I hadn't heard a single word she said.*

"Not at all, I was glad to help her get it back."

"Well, just so you know, they don't make guys like you anymore. Going out of your way to help an elderly lady get her heirloom back is nothing less than an act of chivalry. And by the way, I checked you out. I know who and what you are." My chin rose higher. "Don't worry, can't you tell by the car I drive that I love excitement? Fast cars, bad boys, you know? Don't you just love this sandwich? Here, you've got a little bit of ketchup on your lip."

With her long pointer finger, she wiped the corner of my mouth, found the smudge of red, then slowly placed her finger between her lips, and even more slowly washed it clean with the end of the most sensual tongue I have ever seen.

"There, that's better," she added, leaning in closer and searching my lips for more. Finding none, her fingers ventured lower, lower to the crooked scar that went from ear to ear below my chin. I pulled back just an inch or so. "It's okay, Nicky, it makes you look like a tough guy, you know? Hey, what are you doing tonight, Nicky? Do you have plans?"

"Tonight? Hmmm. I'm not sure yet."

"Would anyone care for dessert?" the waitress asked. "We have homemade carrot cake today."

"Mmmm," Alex moaned. "Maybe just a bite. Trying to watch my figure. How about one piece please, with two forks?"

My cellphone rang; it was Friday again. "Will you

excuse me, Alex? Do you mind if I get this? I'll be right back."

"Not at all, I need to use the ladies' room anyway."

"Hello?"

"It's me."

"What's up?"

"My daughter's kitty made it out of intensive care. He's a tough son of a gun, Skipper. It's going to be a long haul, but it looks like he's going to make it."

"Okay, good. Keep me posted."

"I will. And the woman that sits with the saints still wants you to call her."

"Oh, that's right..., okay..., talk later, bye."

Jessie, I thought. *I can't forget her trial..., yeah, that's this week. Woody Woodward Getz, that's right, he assaulted her..., yeah. Too much on my fuckin' plate!!!*

I made it to the men's room just as I was hanging up. It sounded like I was alone in there, I mean, it was so quiet. The smell of the urinals reminded me of the dumpster and the image of Bobby C laying at the bottom as those maggots scurried across his stoic face. I wanted to puke just thinking about what they did to him.

I peed as fast as I could. Finishing up couldn't have happened quicker. The smell was becoming more nauseating, so I sidestepped some wet spots on the tile floor and put one hand under the automatic soap dispenser, which totally grossed me out when my thumb touched the spigot. I placed both hands under the water faucet, but scrubbing just wouldn't wash my life's stench away.

Suddenly startled, the toilet flushed from inside the stall behind me! In a catlike reflex, my whole body jerked, and I was in a stoop position before I knew it, unsnapping the one clip on my ankle holster and pulling on the .380 by its pearl-handled grips.

I waited and I listened, lifting my PPK out of its holster and up to my calf. *Is it Mountain? Or just as bad, Crazy Carlo?* Whoever it was, I had no idea they were in there, and that bothered me to no end.

Then the stall door burst open like a gate holding a pissed-off bull, ridden by a cowboy with a tight tether wrapped around and pulling on its coglionis. Only it wasn't a bull, it was some over-eaten, satisfied mammalucco (mameluke, ridiculous person) buckling up his oversized, suspended pants, exhaling a few nasty grunts like he'd just delivered a ten-pound baby boy.

Tucking my handgun in my waistband, I stepped aside and waited for the guy to finish up and finally leave before I wrapped my hands in hand towels and leaned on the sink counter– looking deep into the water spotted mirror.

The lines on my face. Where did they come from? I leaned in closer and squinted a long squint. *Oh my God, I'm getting so old. It seems like just yesterday when I was a young Nicky Mancusso, the kid on the block that helped the old widows when they couldn't make their rent at the end of the month, expecting nothing in return but maybe a block of cheese or a pinch on the cheek. I was invincible. Now, I'm in trouble. Lots of trouble. I'm facing possible murder charges if my godson cooperates with the FBI; one of my best soldiers is fighting for his life at St. Mary's Hospital; there is a contract out on me and my crew; and if that isn't enough, my wife isn't speaking to me.*

Leaning on the sink made me realize that I was truly getting old, like an old timer leaning on a walker. *I didn't even know there was someone in that stall. I would never have missed that in the old days. Is that an age spot on my temple? What the Christ.* I ran my fingers under the water, then through my dark brown hair, *still my best attribute*, I thought. *Maybe it's the fluorescent lighting in here? Isn't that what they say?*

A deep breath followed by a long sigh told me it was time to stop the nonsense. *There is a beautiful woman out there, your therapist, for Christ sakes. If I cave in and accept her invitation, the benefits will be immense. Like nothing I've had before. The memories will last a lifetime!*

I stepped back from the mirror and sink, spun around, and punched my closed fist into my open hand. *Don't do it, Nicky. Don't let yourself do it. This time you'll lose Grace forever!* I pushed my fist tighter into my hand and twisted. *Just thank her for lunch and walk away. Just..., walk..., away!*

My cellphone rang as I was leaving the men's room, so I answered as I walked.

"Yeah?"

"Is this the Lone Ranger?"

"Who's this?"

"You know who this is." It was Mountain!

"Hey, gummy bear, you big momo! Long time no see! Seen a dentist lately?"

"Laugh now, dead man, because I promise you, when I'm finished, you'll never laugh again. The war is on, Lone Ranger, and we are coming at you with both barrels. One by one we'll find you, and one by one you will suffer. You'll suffer like your man Bobby did. I gotta say though, he was tough. He wouldn't squeal like a pig when Crazy Carlo prompted him to. But you will, Lone Ranger..., you will!" *Click.*

Still walking, I hung up my phone and looked up. Alex was standing, waiting for me beside our table. It looked like she touched up her makeup but certainly didn't need to. The catlike pencil line in the outer corners of her eyes seemed more pronounced. *She had to have just done that,* I thought.

"Everything okay, Nicholas Francis Mancusso?"

Forcing a smile that ended with an unintentional smirk, I tucked my cell phone into my front pocket. "Everything's fine, Alexandria Elisabeth Pearlmutter."

"Good, because I paid the bill and had them wrap up the carrot cake to go. What do you say we go for a ride to the coast? There's a little bed and breakfast I know of that serves the most scrumptious baked stuffed lobsters–two pounders, and Scorpion Bowls for two after dark. Want to go? No expectations, Nicky," she said with confidence, eye-to-eye, business-like but still seductive.

With the Feds building a case on me for the murder of my best friend Carmine, and the start of the war between Providence and the two renegades in New York, my head was full, full of shit. The last thing I needed was an affair with my super-sexy therapist. I couldn't bear to hurt Grace again, either.

Plus, Star was breathing down my throat ever since she returned to the Cat. And my new friend, Jessie Jayne Calderone had made a connection with me that, well, just felt right. I didn't want to lose that either. I had lots on my plate all right and certainly too much to lose.

It was hard to look into those sexy, hazel eyes and stay focused. But I knew I needed to answer her in a timely fashion, so I tried to put it in a way that wouldn't embarrass her— or me. It came out this way, short and sweet, the only way I knew how.

"No expectations?" I ran my fingers through the right side of my damp hair and stood up straight. "Alright, Alex, let's go. I'll carry the carrot cake, you drive." *It'll never survive,* I thought.

TWELVE

The carrot cake that Alex brought with us was delicious, and getting it "to go" was a good idea. Eating it in the car was another story though. When we left the restaurant, it seemed like that sexy little lipstick-red Porsche, had a mind of her own. I know the driver certainly did.

The drive to Narragansett Beach was fast and furious, or so the saying goes. Maybe my doctor-appointed therapist wanted to show me that she was just as much a "bad girl" as I was a bad boy. In any case, my white knuckles were permanently cast into the top of her dash where I said about three Hail Marys and four Our Fathers.

"Nicky, there's a little bed and breakfast down here by the water's inlet, sometimes bay seals swim up and sun themselves on the large rocks, just off shore. Let's check it out!" Before I had a chance to answer, the stick shift to the right of the most beautiful knee I'd ever seen, slammed into fifth, giving me whiplash for the fourth or fifth time.

"Hey Alex, anyone ever sit in this seat before me and live to tell about it?" I was afraid that my pant leg was riding up and my .380 strapped to my ankle might be showing.

She giggled. "What are you trying to say, sir?"

"Oh nothing, I wouldn't dare!"

"I just think that there isn't anything hotter than fast cars," she said, over the winding of the unmistakable, high-pitched European engine. "Although, outlaws come in a close second!"

We made more bullshit conversation, while she did most of the talking, which was most of the time. I didn't care though. With a girl like her, you didn't need ears, just eyes.

"Nicky, can I ask you something?" she blurted, as she gently scratched just above that incredible knee with nails that looked too good to be real. I knew exactly what it was. What she was going to ask me, I mean. Been there, done that. They usually wait until they think we are tight, confidants, brethren—and sometimes it could be just hours after we've met too. They're all the same. She was going to ask me something about the "life." I guess they think that by asking, and by me answering– that lets them in, even if just a little. Enough to give them a sense of empowerment. Only, with this one, I think it was more like a turn-on. If they are timid, they will use the word, "Mob," but if they are either bold or stupid, they'll use the word "Mafia." *Let's see what this one does,* I thought.

My usual response. "Sure Alex, you can ask me anything," acting surprised.

"Is it true? Are you everything they say you are?"

"Like what? Am I a hard-working guy?"

"Um..., no."

"Oh." I relaxed my grip on the dashboard a little. "Do you mean am I loyal to my friends?"

"Um..., not that either," she giggled, as she downshifted to fourth, then back into fifth, forcing me to tighten my grip again. The giggle reminded me that she'd had a glass of wine with her burger. She continued. "I want to know...,"

Holy shit, I thought. *They usually drag the sentence out like that only after we've...* "I just want to know," she said slowly, her Porsche winding out in third as she downshifted instead of using the brake, confirming it *was* the wine.

"What's it like to...," *Here it comes,* I thought. "Um..., never mind," she continued. "I'll save it for our sessions. We have plenty of time for curiosities. Here's the bed n' breakfast, Nicky– up on the right, isn't it endearing?"

Endearing, I thought. *Endearing, Grace uses that word. She uses it with me. She uses it with my Heather and with Little Carmine. I never heard anyone say it until I met Grace. Endearing.*

The high rev of the sports car slowly unwound as we pulled into a spot facing the water. *Romantic,* I thought. I wondered how many times she'd been there before.

Exhaling slowly through my nose I sat still, still holding onto the dashboard with my right hand.

Alex threw open her door, fast, but exited slow, as if she were performing a well-choreographed dance, a sexy and most erotic dance. Her legs lifted her expensive, and no doubt name-brand heels, exposing the most impeccably-smooth and tanned thighs as they left the vehicle. I was gawking and she knew it. As she twisted in her seat, her right leg followed her left, in the same timely manner as if practiced a thousand times before. She was by far the most desirable woman I've ever met. Yet, I just sat there. Motionless, still holding onto the dash like a scared little boy.

"Alex," I called out, closing my eyes, as a whiff of her intoxicating fragrance drifted over me, as fresh air entered the vehicle, signaling me to shit or get off the pot.

"Yes?" she answered, seductively, very seductively. I took a slow and deliberate breath.

"Alex, I can't do this. I..., I just can't. I'm sorry. Please, please take me back?" Bowing my head, I felt about two feet tall.

"Take you back? Are you okay? Did I make you carsick with my crazy driving?"

"No, no, it's not that. It's not that at all. It's just that..., I..., I love my wife. I'm sorry," I said, head still stooped.

She tapped the little roof of her little car, one fingernail at a time, starting with her pinky finger and ending with her pointer.

"Sorry?" she hollered back from outside the car, standing there, holding on to the roof line, her lower half facing me through the opened door. She began banging on the Porsche's roof, rings and nails clinking and clicking as her opened hands slapped the metal top – then bent down to see me, eye to eye.

"You're sorry! Are you kidding me? Nicky! Sorry!" Still holding on to the roof's edge, she squatted further before continuing.

"That was one of the bravest things I've ever seen anyone ever do. You're sorry? Oh my God, if there were only more people with your sense of loyalty! Oh, I'll take you back alright, but now I want you more than ever!" She giggled, girlish-like, still looking at me face to face, oozing with so much sex appeal!

"But I'm not giving up! I'm not!" she announced. "I'm hot and I'm not! Your wife is a very lucky woman, Nicholas Mancusso, very lucky!"

I remained quiet as she moved quickly, plopping back down into her seat, adjusting the rear-view mirror to check her perfect hair and makeup. As we backed out of the lot, Alex continued to speak.

"Nicky, as I'm sure you can tell, I've got my vices, and lots of them, but I also have my dreams–and maybe someday I'll take my own advice and learn to quell the fire burning inside of me, enough to attract a guy like you. What you did was a very hard thing to do. You should be very proud of yourself, mister."

"Yeah, right. I don't feel very proud right now.

My friends would never believe it if I told them. Thanks for the kind words though. Take me back now? There's something I gotta do."

"Sure, let's go." The ride back was slower and calmer, as if Alex, me, and the sports car were now in sync.

Alex pulled into her reserved parking space and released me. And I was glad. On the way back, I listened to the radio– a song called The Dance, by Garth Brooks. My wife Grace was at the forefront of my mind and I welcomed the temporary distraction.

When I got to the hospital, Grace was sitting by Carla's bed, serene, polite, clutching her rosary in one hand. She hadn't seen me yet.

There were tubes and lines everywhere, criss-crossed, messed up with uneven and sporadic white tape, holding things down anywhere and everywhere.

The beeps from the trees of bags and the unreadable monitors seemed to bounce off each other, and I wondered how anyone could distinguish what beep or blip was for what. Carla's eyes were closed, as she lay there in bed like a corpse. Each eyelid sporting the color of light purple, contrasted against her pastel and waxy facial skin. She looked terrible.

But there was my Grace. The woman I loved, holding Carla's hand with love in her eyes, looking so..., so..., endearing.

Not to startle her, I waited in the doorway for her to look up and see me. It took a few moments but she did, and when she did, the story in her eyes told it all.

Grace told many stories with her eyes. She always did. The story she was telling then invited me to step toward her, so I did.

She stood to speak, speak with just her eyes. Looking into hers, I told her how much I loved her–with mine. Her eyes said the same back to me. Grace taught me that a 20 second hug releases endorphins or something like that. I pretend to count because I know that she does. I do think it works though because I always feel much better afterward.

"How's Carla doing?" I asked, softly, caringly, on my best behavior.

"I don't know, she's stable but she's emotionally wounded too. She lost a lot of blood trying to slit her wrists. But she comes and goes, waking up at times, calling for her son, Nicholas." I think Grace felt funny mentioning his name, after what he did to me.

"Oh, Nicky, poor Carla– it has to be unbearable

losing both your husband and your son. I know Nicholas is still alive, but not being able to see him since he's been locked up in that federal army barracks gives Carla no hope at all. She needs hope, Nicky!"

"Army barracks? Did she say where, Grace? I'm just curios in case it's close by, maybe we could arrange a visit for her?" *I'll find that piece of shit,* I thought.

"I don't know, that would be great though. Once she awoke and babbled something about wanting to go to Fort Devens, I think. If we could get the authorities to let Carla see her son, that would be awesome! Do you think you could arrange it, honey? Will you try?"

"Let me step out and make a quick phone call. I know someone that may be able to help. I'll be right back."

The waiting room was full of sorry souls. A young couple sat arm in arm, two teenage girls were engaged in their cell phones, and an elderly lady held on to black rosary beads herself as if someone was going to take them from her. I found a quiet corner and dialed.

"Hey, it's me. Listen, Mrs. Marchetti still has that bird (code for the FBI still has Nicholas) the one she's trying to get to sing. Someone said she sent the bird away for singing lessons to that place where the little guy used to live, you know, when he was young, like eighteen? Ask the little guy, *capische*? Go through No Neck. Right, bye."

When the boss was old enough, he was drafted into the army and spent six weeks at Fort Devens before being shipped off to Korea. Years ago, I saw a picture of him and a small group of young soldiers hanging on the wall in his office. I asked Santini about it, but I could tell he didn't want to talk much about it. He mentioned Fort Devens but when I asked about Korea all he said was, "Six of us posed for that picture and only two of us lived to view it."

Grace was anxiously waiting by the door when I returned. "Did you have any luck, Nicky?" Were you able to get Carla to visit Nicholas? That would so lift her spirits."

"I'm trying to get her to, Grace, I'm trying really hard."

"Excuse me, Mrs. Mancusso?" the doctor on call interrupted, ignoring me, which I didn't like.

"Yes," Grace answered. "Did Carla's test results come back?"

"They did," he answered, still ignoring me. "It

seems she's suffering from something consistent with rat poisoning. We found high levels of arsenic along with a pesticide in her blood."

"Oh, God," Grace said, grabbing my arm to hold herself up. I chimed in, uninvited.

"What did she do, sprinkle it on her corn flakes, Doc?"

"Uh, not exactly," he replied, not amused. It wasn't she who ate the pesticide. You see, we found a partially digested rat in her stomach."

"You mean the rat ate that shit and then Carla ate the rat? Now, that's different," I replied.

Grace dry heaved with a force, moving toward the waste basket in the corner of the room. "Nick..., Nicky!" she whispered, grabbing and squeezing my arm in between violent yet silent heaves.

"We believe that Mrs. Torro is suffering from mental illness," the doctor continued. "Our psychiatric team evaluated her and found that she is quite overwhelmed with the recent incarceration of her son, Nicholas. Our team also learned that her husband was murdered?"

"Yes, about seven years ago," I replied.

Grace interjected, wiping the corners of her

mouth, although nothing was there to wipe, then continued.

"Carla's husband, Carmine, was savagely butchered by an animal. An animal without a soul. The sick monster cut her husband's throat then forced a dead parrot into his mouth, leaving his wife and children to find him that wa..." Grace stopped in mid-sentence, looking sternly into the doctor's eyes. "Birds and rats are sent as messages to others that are contemplating singing like a bird or telling on your friends like a rat. Do you think that is why Carla ate the rat? Oh, Nicky..., I can't take any more of this craziness," she sobbed, turning to me for much-needed support. "Poor Carla, poor sweet Carla. She doesn't deserve any of this!"

"I know she doesn't, Grace. Here, sit down. Doctor, do you think Carla is eating rats because of the way her husband was found?"

"It is quite possible, Mr. Mancusso. Either way, Mrs. Torro is going to need a lot of help in dealing with her issues."

"Well, she can count on my wife and me," I said, turning to my wife. "Grace, honey, I have to leave you. I have that thing I have to attend to."

The look that she gave me was intense, more than

serious, but I'd seen it before. I leaned over her and kissed her forehead, then the bridge of her nose, then her lips, cupping both of her cheeks with my hands and fingers. I froze for a brief second before pulling away, as the image of Alex's face appeared before my closing eyes, then morphed back into Grace's as I opened them.

"I have to go; we'll talk tonight when I get home. I love you, honey. Goodbye doctor, thank you for taking care of our friend."

I never looked back for a response, already knowing it.

Pushing hard on the elevator button didn't get the door to open any faster, but I pressed down hard just the same. As I jumped inside, a couple of young, nervous-acting, gangsta-rapper weirdoes were already eyeing me for a weakness. Before the doors closed, I could smell what they were up to.

The sideways, square-top, light green ball caps and the lighter green headbands underneath, clashed grotesquely with the lime-green, plastic-looking pants they had hanging below their crotches. If they tied their oversized and goofy sneakers, I might have taken them more seriously but their getup was just too stupid.

As we approached floor number two, they asked me if I had any money. And, landing on floor number one, I explained to them their mistake. When the doors slid open to the lobby, I gave a quick glance back at them while leaving the elevator. Both wanna-be gangstas were on the floor, sitting on their useless asses, rubbing their useless heads underneath their side-ways, useless ball caps. The doors closed on them again and took them for a ride to who knows where.

THIRTEEN

I made it to the municipal parking lot at the courthouse just in time to find the last open space. Remembering to leave my Walther PPK underneath the seat was more like habit rather than a miracle. Metal detectors had been my enemy a few times when I was a much younger wise guy.

The smug guard, full of mustache, operated that security machine like it was his only calling in life. As I went through the metal detector, I was tempted to ask him if he had ever smiled but instead forced myself to "can it" and not press my luck. *They were just like I had remembered them. Mean, with no personality.*

The courtroom was packed with suits. Most sitting on the defendant's side. I couldn't tell if they were professionals or family; either way that showed me the status of the accused.

Behind the prosecutor's table sat family and friends of the victim, the working class. I slipped in and sat unnoticed behind them.

I spotted Jessie Jayne from behind, she looked small. *Turn around,* I said, but only in my mind. *Turn around, see me!*

"Hear ye, hear ye, please rise, the court is now in session. The honorable Judge Stevens will preside."

Turn around, Jessie, I'm here! I screamed silently, one more time, as she slowly rose with the others, still facing front.

Then, as if I commanded it, she clenched her hands together and pressed them against her chest like she was consoling herself, and nervously turned and laid her frightened eyes upon mine.

She smiled but only with her eyes. It was enough for me.

The bailiff was full of mustache too and bellowed an old-fashioned bellow, "You may be seated!" But Jessie wasn't ready to be.

Her attorney tugged on her a little, while her head tilted and her eyes leaked a small "thank you" to me on her way down. My smiling eyes said "you're welcome," then I slowly sat to try to get her to do the same.

After all the courtroom formalities and the charges were read, the trial got underway. The attorney for Woodrow "Woody" Getz rose to address the jury.

"Good afternoon ladies and gentlemen, my name is Kirk Van Houten III." I wanted to puke. The attorney was a pompous fat-cat with a vocabulary that made you want to choke those condescending and everlasting vowels and consonants right out of his guttural throat.

After each and every sentence, whether it called for it or not, he said the word, "okay?" But he pronounced it like this, "*Ow-kai*"? It was like nails running down a chalkboard each time he said it.

The only thing worse was Getz himself. He sat there with the most repulsive and cockiest smirk on his face the whole time! I think it was his permanent look, and he didn't know how to appear remorseful or innocent. Maybe he just didn't care.

My blood was boiling just watching him, so I had to look away. Instead, I focused on sweet Jessie Jayne, throwing all good thoughts at her while saying a Hail Mary prayer for her while I sat. I must say, I did pretty good. I managed to stay in my seat as Kirk Van Douche Bag tore Jessie's story and reputation apart, bit by bit, lying through his teeth about his client's innocence. By the time the judge called it a day, Jessie was visibly shaken, breaking my heart in the process.

I met her in the lobby as she and her attorney pushed the parking garage elevator button.

"Thank you so much for coming, Nicky. It means so much to me."

"I wouldn't miss supporting you Jessie Jayne, wild horses couldn't keep me away. I've got to run though, my friend. I'll try to make it back here again, okay?" Immediately I thought of Van Douche bag's "*ow-kai*?" I hoped I didn't say it like that. "I'll talk to you soon."

"Goodbye, Nicky. Thank you!"

"You're welcome. Bye, Jess."

I rushed back to where else, St. Mary's Hospital again. This time, to quickly visit with Bobby C. I hadn't seen him since those two New York guys, Crazy Carlo and Mountain kidnapped and performed a thing called buckwheats on him. They shot him up his rectum with a small caliber bullet, leaving him to die a slow and agonizing death at the bottom of a maggot infested dumpster behind the Pink Pussy Cat Gentlemen's Club.

And now they hunted the rest of me and my crew.

I wasn't able to visit Bobby sooner because of the

heat brought on by the Nicholas Torro thing and needed to keep a low profile.

Sick and tired of that damn hospital, I still managed to march in to Bobby's room with an upbeat attitude.

"Skipper!" Friday Night hollered out, as he poured a cup of water from the pink, plastic pitcher on a roll-away table by Bobby's bed.

"How you doin', Friday?"

"Good, Skipper, good. Still trying to get this guy out of this friggin' bed." After a quick kiss on the cheek from Friday, he stepped aside so I could get in close to see Bobby. There was no way I could easily reach to kiss him, not with all the wires and hoses surrounding him, so I held his hand instead.

"Hey Bobby, you hangin' in there?" I reached in as far as I could get.

"I'm trying, Skipper. This guy over here is hovering over me like a mother hen, though. Can you take him with you when you leave?"

"I'm the best nurse you've ever had," Friday barked back, from behind the chrome trees full of hanging bags, lines, and small display screens.

"Hey Skipper," Bobby asked, we gonna get those guys?"

"I'm working on it, "Brother."

"Skipper, I mean, before they get us, you know? They are some nasty guys, man. They enjoy torturing, they really do! They get off on it! I think they are going rogue too, because I overheard them when they got a call from their street boss in New York! They told their captain every lie in the book, Skipper. I don't think he's in on any of this. In fact, I overheard them say that they had better hurry up and ditch my body, because if the boss knows that they made a hit without permission they just as soon bury their own bodies too."

"After they dropped me into that dumpster, Skipper, they told me I'd have company real soon, because they were going after the rest of our crew, one by one. They said, they were "going to the mattresses!" You know what that means! We really pissed them off, Skipper!"

"Yeah well, our families haven't gone to the mattresses in years, and I'm not about to let that happen if I can help it. You just worry about getting better, Bobby. I'm going to let the rest of the guys visit you two at a time, now that the dust has settled. Let Nurse Lover Boy here help you to get out of here, I need you back."

"Will do, Skip. And, by the way, thanks for finding me. The maggots were becoming tiresome company. There was one I liked but she was taken."

"Don't mention it, Bobby. See you in a few days."

Before I left, I called Friday Night out into the corridor for a talk.

"What's up, Skipper?"

I just wanted to let you know, that when the books open up, I'm going to propose you to be a "made guy." You've made your bones more than once, and once is all you need. I think you are ready.

"Are you serious, Skip? I don't know what to say.

"Say nothing. Let's just live through this thing first, *capisce*?"

"Thank you, Skipper." We hugged, then kissed."

"Alright, get that guy in there back to our crew ASAP."

"Will do, Nicky. Thank you."

The term "making bones" means proving yourself by doing something serious to gain respect.

You cannot become "Made" unless you've participated in "wacking." This way you won't rat on your family because you have "dirty hands" yourelf.

FOURTEEN

After stopping by my shop for a few things, I headed for the club. My cell phone rang a split second before thinking my cell phone hadn't rung. It was Iron Mike.

"Hello?"

"Nicky, they almost got Brandon."

"What?"

"Brandon, those two stooges almost got Brandon! He was coming out of his apartment and luckily, he spotted New York plates. He hit the ground just in time when all hell broke loose. A hail of gunfire went right over his head before they sped off. What do you want to do?"

"Have everyone meet me at the diner. Everyone! One hour."

"Right, Skipper."

I arrived a few minutes late after stopping by the club first. I needed the boss's advice on one thing, information on a second thing, and his blessing on the third. I got two out of the three.

They were all waiting for me at the diner. "Iron Mike" Tessoni, "Friday Night" Carella, Brandon and Brendon Sacoccia, Tony "Jackpot" Canatta, Tommy "Gag" Gaglione, and even "No Neck" Nunzio.

Needing a warrant to do so first, the Feds didn't have enough time to plant a bug at the diner, so we were safe. Also, for security, I had Jimmy the Weasel's guys, Ronnie T and Jay, stand guard outside during the meeting, just in case any unwelcomed guests dropped in.

"How you doin', alright?" I asked Brandon, as he was the last to greet me. "

"I'm alright, Skipper, just a little shaken up."

"Good. Alright, I'll get right down to it." I turned my cell phone on vibrate and threw it on the table, had everyone do the same. Then I turned over two bowls and covered the phones with them, something I'd learned from my underboss, Billy Bath, before he was beheaded by those psychos Jonny Moonlight and Lieutenant Howie Bergle.

As I've said many times before, Bergle made great

fertilizer for the boss's tomato plants and Moonlight helped feed the lions at Roger Williams Park Zoo. Bergle's cogliones still sit proudly atop a shelf in Santini's office.

I proceeded. "As you all know, we've got a small problem. Those two New York chooches are not backing off, not until they get us all. Well, us, meaning all that were there the night they stuck Lucky's head in that vice and we sent them home looking like that monster on Rudolph the Red Nosed Reindeer. On their escort back across state lines, I had Iron Mike force the two rogue guys to bite down on the route 95 guardrail. Then, Mikey's size 14 boot kicked down on the back of their heads, collecting a hand full of ivory for the tooth fairy.

"The Abominable Snowman," Brendon piped in.

"What?" I asked.

The monster, it was the Abominable Snowman," he repeated. All gums, he laughed, before I gave him a look.

"Whatever. Anyway, Tony..., you, Nunzio and Tommy might be safe, I don't know. The boss is currently reaching out to New York to try to figure out if this is an all-out war between the families' thing or just two rogue soldiers going behind their boss's back. Either way, we can't wait. We need to act and act fast. Being picked off one by one is something we're not going to sit by and watch happen.

Just then, Ronnie T interrupted by poking his head in from around the corner by the doorway entrance.

"Nicky," Ronnie shouted, with his hand cupped over his mouth, twice, I think. Being interrupted like that set everyone's alarm bells off. It seemed like each one of us either tapped their ankle, back-belt or side arm and shifted in their seats all at the same time.

"What is it, Ronnie?"

"Sorry to bother you, but there's a woman here to see you. She says it's urgent."

Oh, Christ, who now? What now?

"Hold on, Ronnie, I'll be right there." *Christ,* I thought. "Guys, give me a second, will ya? I'll blow off whoever it is, let me just make sure everyone's alright." *Who the hell? Because of her connection to the club, Star would be the only woman I know who could find me here.*

Dodging the other tables and chairs, I made my way with Ronnie and the entranceway. The look on his face was weird. I looked at him as if to say, "Who the hell is it?" But he just shrugged his shoulders and stepped out of the way in order for me to go first.

As I rounded the corner, I was taken back. In fact, it took me a second to take it in. I was confused. She didn't belong there, not in that world, not in that life of mine. But there she stood, looking confident yet somewhat timid.

"Hello, Nicky. I'm sure you're surprised to see me."

"What are you doing here, Alex?"

"I'm sorry but I had to come. I need to speak with you, it's urgent."

"What's wrong? Just tell me, "I replied, annoyed that my phone was vibrating away in my front pocket, but no way was I going to answer it. I just had to know what possessed my therapist to seek me out and interrupt a meeting I was in, knowing the kind of business I conduct.

"Is there somewhere we can talk, Nicky? Can I wait for you until your meeting is over? I promise I'll be quiet until then. Just buy me a diet Coke and let me wait in the corner until you're done, I promise I'll be quiet. Please it's urgent!"

"Alex, what can be so important that it can't wait..., hold on, this damn phone in my pocket is vibrating nonstop..., hold..." Then it hit me. It hit me like a ton of bricks! I had taken my cell phone out of my pocket and left it on the table, under a bowl. And, cell phones don't vibrate nonstop, but bug detecting devices do. Especially the kind of bug detecting device that you clip onto your keychain, then forget about it after your suave attorney gives it to you as a gift. And boy, what a gift it was.

But as the thought of betrayal entered my mind, the blood ran from my head, leaving me feeling instantly lightheaded and weak.

Alex Elizabeth Pearlmutter, the sexiest and most beautiful girl I knew, had betrayed me. And I never saw it coming.

As the bug detector vibrated undetected in my pocket, Alex spoke, but I never heard a word. I just saw visions of what was yet to come. I was heartbroken! She was wired!

"Skipper, are you okay? I'm going to get you a glass of water. You look a little pale," Ronnie said, as he turned to Alex in an attempt to excuse my lack of answering her when she spoke. And still, the vibrator vibrated continuously in my pocket.

"It must be the caffeine in my coffee," I said, as I got my wits about me. "I'll be okay." I took the glass of water from Ronnie T and sipped on it slowly. I'd been punched in the gut before but not that hard and not by a girl. "Alex, wait here a second. Ronnie keep my friend company for a minute."

"Will do, Nicky."

My trip back to the table was eternal. I had to tip my guys off to the bug but needed to speak in code.

"Friday," I began, slowly, very slowly. That meant something is up so pay attention.

"Mrs. Marchetti, the *fica nasa*, just came in, *andiamo*." That meant, the FBI is here, listening, let's go.

I continued. "We're moving the meeting to the other place." That meant Helen's. "Thirty Minutes," I said.

"Got it," Friday announced, quietly. "Okay guys, let's break it up. *Statazit*," he said (*sta-ta-zeet*, shut up) on the way out, *capische*?"

No one answered, just moved quickly and quietly. I didn't even look at the guys; I just grabbed my phone from under the bowl on the table and walked back over to Alex.

I listened to some bullshit sob story about her mom and the landlord that's giving her trouble about paying her rent and keeping her dog. *Are you kidding me? Does she think I'm stupid? She stole that bullshit scenario right out of the Godfather Part II movie. Do the Feds really think I don't watch movies?*

I listened, nodded, and listened some more. And when she was done, I walked her to the lipstick red Porsche, told her I would see what I could do and closed the car door for her after she got in. As she drove away, that's when the device on my keychain stopped vibrating. And that's when my desire for her did too.

FIFTEEN

Consumed with thoughts of Alex, I pushed through to the meeting with my crew. We all met at Helen's Restaurant at about the same time and began where we left off. The guys pretended that the Alex thing never happened. They knew better. I began this way.

"Guys, Bobby's in the hospital with a broken body. Brendon was shot at and almost wasted. We are not going to wait for another strike."

"But what about the danger of starting a war?" Iron Mike asked.

"Let me worry about that, Mikey. We gotta do what we gotta do. We're going to the mattresses. Tell your wives you'll be away for a while. Everyone stay close. Eat, sleep, and shit together. Choose a location, I don't care where, and live amongst yourselves.

Going to the mattresses goes back to the days of Sicily and it is part of La Cosa Nostra. It works. When the plan is formulated, you'll be informed, so sit tight, stay out of the public eye, and be very, very careful. And no Gumadas for a while. If you can't see your wives, you certainly can't see your Gumadas. Bunk together and hunker down. Stay safe."

You could have heard a pin drop.

"Alright next. That Nicholas Torro thing. We know where the Feds are hiding him. He's not in a maximum or even minimum prison; he's not even in a jail. They're treating the would-be killer as if he's on vacation in a resort. Friday, get word to this crumb out of respect for his father, Carmine."

"If he gets amnesia about us, tell him he'll get a one-time pass. We won't come after him. Of course, he'll have to swallow a prison sentence for what he did to me and disappear when he gets out. Forever. But if he doesn't take this one-time deal and squeals to the Feds, his life won't be worth a nickel. He's got two days to make a decision."

"Okay, Skipper. How will I get word to him?" Friday asked.

"Go see his uncle Vincent. You know who he is,

Carla's brother. Don't let on that we know where the kid is."

"Done," he said.

"Mikey, you come with me. I've got a job for you. The rest of you stay in one room, eat, sleep, and get to know each other like a tick on a dog. Stay low and don't forget to look under your vehicles."

After my private sit-down with Mikey, I headed home for a long and overdue talk with Grace. Pulling into my driveway I felt uneasy this time. For some reason I glanced over at the old neighbor's house, hoping it was manned with fifty armed federal agents, but there was just old Mrs. Battista and her cat, Michelangelo.

Grace must have heard me coming, because she opened the front door without a care in the world, which immediately got me going. I did my best not to show my concern though.

"Nicky? You're home early. I wish I knew you were coming; I'd of cooked a meal for you. I have left-over macaroni in the fridge. Did you eat? Do you want some?"

"No thank you, Grace. Actually, well, maybe just a small plate while we talk."

"Talk?"

"Talk. I'd like to talk." I followed her to the kitchen and sat as she searched the fridge. Of course, I glanced at the utility closet before settling in. The ghost of Carmine lived behind that door and there's nothing I could do about it.

"Talk about what, Nicky?"

"About Star. And her daughter, Nicki. It's been the elephant in the room ever since you met her. Am I right, Grace? Don't you want to ask me something?"

"Well, now that you mention it. Yes, I would like to ask you something."

"Ask away, let's end this here and now."

She slid a container of ziti onto the counter. The gravy was in a separate container and had meatballs and sweet Italian sausage in it. I liked it better the second time around, because the gravy soaked into the lines on the macaroni overnight and tasted better heated up again.

"Alright," she said, eyes looking down and away, timid, and gentle, just like the girl I fell for all those years ago. Grace was the kind of girl that you take home to mom. That's what I wanted then, and that's what I wanted now. All the Stars and Moons, the Jessie Jaynes and the Alexs can come and go, but they meant nothing to me compared to Grace.

In the mob culture, a lot of guys have a Gumada or two on the side, and that's okay, as long as they don't forget about their wives. Especially the mother of their children. They must cherish them and honor them, but most of all, put them above the Gumada.

Some wives accept the mistress as long as they know they come first. Friday night is Gumada night, but come Saturday night, you had better take your wife out to a more expensive restaurant, and never, ever, bring them both to the same establishment.

The ultimate insult to your wife is when the maître d' tells her "It's nice to see you again" and he sits you at your "usual table," especially if it's the first time the wife has been there.

For me, I don't need it. I find that they just get in the way of business. That's partly why I am a good Capo.

"Go for it, Grace," I said. Ask away."

"Okay Nicky, I will. Tell me, how do you know Star?"

"I'll answer that," I said, leaning forward with both hands and arms on the table. "Star was in some trouble a few years back, about seven years or so I guess. And I helped her to get away and start a new life. Next question?"

"Um..., why is her daughter Nicki named after you. The seven-year-old. Why, Nicky? Did you have an affair with Star?"

"Grace," I said, rapping lightly on the table with my knuckles. "I did not have an affair with Star. All I did was help her start a new life. She evidently appreciated that and named her kid after me." I stopped the knuckle rapping. "That's all there is to it, Grace. I promise you."

"Do you swear to God? You know it's a mortal sin if you swear to God, right Nicky? You do remember mortal sins, right?"

"Grace, yes, I remember mortal sins, and, yes, I swear to God. I did not have an affair with Star, okay?"

"Something's not right here, Nicky. I can just feel it. I feel it deep inside me." She went back to heating up more food with eyes looking downward again.

"Listen, honey. Every once in a while, we have these talks. And every once in a while, you get these crazy ideas. They are all in your head, okay? Now come on, have a glass of wine with me while I eat." She reached for the orange soda. I usually didn't drink, but if I occasionally had a glass of wine with my pasta, I always mixed half of it with orange soda.

Something I'd done since I was a kid, when my grandfather put it in front of me at Sunday dinners on Federal Hill. I was seven or eight.

"Now let's forget all these crazy thoughts. Come on, sit with me." My phone rang and made me jump! Instinctively, I glanced over at the utility closet! Grace saw me do it, I just knew it! Before I answered, I walked into the foyer and cleared my throat in order to speak softly.

"Hello?"

"It's me, Nicky. It's Lucky. How you doin', alright? Jackpot said you're looking for me?"

"Yeah, I am. How's your new blue eyeball? Never mind, I don't care. I need to meet with you, Lucky. I need to meet you tonight. I'm gonna come by your house around six. Tell your sister, Phyllis, to have that ankle biter, Fluffy, put away. I can't stand the constant yipping from that thing. I don't know how you people stand it. It gives me a headache."

"It's Lovey," Lucky replied.

"Huh?"

"It's Lovey, the dog's name is Lovey."

"Listen to me Lucky, you degenerate asshole! I don't give a shit if that little bastard's name is Toto,

Poochie, or little asshole! Just have it put away before I get there, got it?"

"Yeah, I got it."

"Good. See you at six."

I dialed my phone as I walked. "Hey, I'm meeting him at six. Right."

I hung up and walked back into the kitchen. My meal was on the table, but there was only one glass of wine. Mine.

"One more question," Grace said, "then I'm all done for the night. Will you answer one more?"

"One more, that's it! Make it good, Grace! Please!" There was already a piece of sausage on my fork so instead of waiting for her to finish speaking, I also stabbed two pieces of ziti and put it all into my mouth, even though I knew Grace wouldn't like it. But I was tired and had more important things on my mind.

"Go ahead, ask," I sloppily and rudely said, chewing with my mouth open, as if to put no validity in her oncoming question at all.

"Why do you glance at the utility closet at times? You've done it over the years, especially when you're stressed or sense danger. Something as little as a phone call can set it off. Does it have something to do with Carmine's death and the way they found him in his?

"You never spoke about his son Nicholas and the attack he made on your life. I guess it's my fault. I really never wanted to know the details. Nicholas was hiding in that closet when he lunged at you wasn't he?"

"Okay, Grace. That was your last question, and here is my last answer." I stabbed at another piece of sausage, then a single macaroni. "If you saw me glance at the utility closet, it was just a coincidence. I don't do that. Now that's it for tonight. No more questions." I drank down the remnants of Father Mario's homemade wine and wiped my mouth with a napkin printed with lady bugs, a Grace thing for sure.

"Thank you, honey, that was delicious as usual. I have to go out now. Please don't wait up." I kissed her cheek and ran upstairs to get ready. She didn't say a word.

SIXTEEN

The club was busier than usual. In fact, I even had a hard time finding a parking space which was unusual for that time of the day. I think the look of the dancers had a lot to do with it. If the girls were hot, then the patrons would come, but if they were plain, they would move on to the next strip joint, usually "The Gazelle" or "The Silver Lake Gentlemen's Club." We get cash tribute payments from each club, so we didn't mind.

Scammy saw me coming and had a club soda ready for me, as I walked by the bar towards the back room. I passed it up.

"Nicky!" a familiar voice hollered, as I made my way through the crowd and past the stage. There was no need to look up, it was clearly Star's voice. So,

I pretended not to hear her and pushed on to the office. The way-back office.

As usual, a card game was in full swing. I could tell it had been going on for a while, by the amount of cigar smoke that hung in the air.

Bruno Lucetti saw me coming and opened the boss's door. He got permission for me to enter, shook my hand, and stepped out of my way. A man of few words. That's what made him a good underboss.

The boss's office was dark and dingy as usual. An open game of solitaire was spread out on the old mahogany desk and his World's Fair ashtray was overfull.

"Come here, Nicola," he mumbled, through the burnt-out stogie hanging out the corner of his mouth. "Come here." I stepped over an old worn-out hassock and reached down to kiss his cheek. *He's getting shorter,* I thought. *Shrinking in his old age.*

The thought of him getting so old brought on a rush of sadness and caught me off guard. It overcame me but was quickly squelched by the sight of Bruno eyeing me down from the open doorway. I would never show a weakness, any weakness, to anyone. Ever.

"What brings you here to see me? Please, sit. Have

a glass of anisette. Bruno, close the door, pour us a glass of anisette."

"No thank you, Antonio. Thank you. I uh..., I need your blessing."

"I'm listening. Speak," he said, taking the small glass from Bruno's hand.

"Well, it's like this. My crew and I, we are going to the mattresses," I said, looking over to Bruno who had a look of surprise and disapproval on his face. "Hopefully it will end as quickly as it begins."

The old man took the stogie from his lips and held on to it as he noticeably spoke with his hands. "And you're asking for my blessing on such a dangerous journey? One that you feel can end quickly? You feel you have this power over two families?"

He put the cigar back between his lips before continuing. "Our two families have lived in peace before you came through this door, Nicky. Why should I now jeopardize this peace?"

I took a deep breath before answering. "Antonio Santini, you are a wise man. You are head of the most powerful family in New England, and your fingers stretch even further beyond. Two rogue members of one of the five families in New York has disrespected us by what they did to Bobby Castratoro, one of your most loyal soldiers. They have vowed to take out more members of your family, including me, your most loyal Capo."

"I ask you for permission to do whatever needs to be done to protect our family."

"My dear and most loyal Capo. You will drink anisette with me, tell me what needs to be done, and I will hear you. In the end I will make my decision, and you will abide by that decision. You took an oath to obey, and that is what you will do. Bruno, pour him a glass of anisette." He held his wet glass high and then touched it to mine. "*Cinzano*," he said, softly but proudly, to which Bruno and I repeated.

"*Cinzano*!" (one hundred years, pronounced *Chin Zon*). "I will now listen," Antonio Santini declared.

As I left the office and made my way through the card tables, I felt surprised at the boss's decision, still thinking of the conversation.

The music was loud and made it hard to concentrate. Before I knew it, I was moving slowly through the crowded stage area and was abruptly stopped in my tracks, as I came face to face with none other than Star herself. She was on duty. Boy, was she on duty. The outfit she had on was wild. There had to be ten or twelve guys and even girls encircling us, checking her out as she stood tall before me with her eight-inch stiletto heels.

I'd heard of "assless or cheekless chaps" and have seen images of them in movies, but never really saw them in person. Until then. And holy shit! They were something to see. Star looked like she was poured into those things and moved like she knew it.

"Nicky Mancusso!" she yelled, over the DJ's lousy pick of what he called music. "Where have you been? I have been back from Florida way too long, and you promised we'd spend time together! Even my daughter Nicki has been asking me when we are going to see you! Where have you been? You can't be that busy!"

"Star," I answered, grasping her hand and pulling her off to the side and away from her gawking fans. "If you only knew. Listen, I can't talk to you, even now. I have somewhere to be. I promise, I'll be in touch. I'll call you."

"You better! I'll hunt you down Nicholas Mancusso until you do!" With that, she slowly turned away, and on purpose I'm sure, exposing her two heart-shaped butt-cheeks through those ass-chaps and walked into the growing sea of onlookers. I headed to Lucky's house.

SEVENTEEN

I told Lucky I'd be there at six, and I was right on time. I was curious to see if he had Phyllis put that damn ankle-biter away, like I asked. I was in no mood to hear its constant yapping right then.

Exiting my truck was hairy. If Mountain and Crazy Carlo were going to pick us off, it would be going in or coming out of our frequented places.

As I walked across the street and up the walkway, I could imagine hearing Mountain calling me, Lone Ranger, and telling me when he was done with me, I would know what it means to suffer.

I imagined having to endure something like buckwheats, like Bobby C did. *Frig that! I do not want to experience it!* One shot up the ass, not immediately lethal, but causing massive damage to the bowels and digestive system is not my cup of tea. The buckwheats method prolongs life, just long enough for the sufferer to experience a lengthy and most agonizing, infectious death.

As I rang the doorbell, I looked toward the driveway where Lucky's car was not. I recalled the maggots crawling hungrily across Bobby's face, itching his tortured skin while he lay paralyzed among bathroom trash. I think my nostrils still bore the smell of the rancid food parts from the Pink Pussy Cat's rat-ridden dumpster.

"Phyllis is in the basement, Nicky," Vernon said, holding the front door open for me while stroking, Fluffy. "Lucky said he wanted to meet with you downstairs, so he asked Phyllis to set up a bridge table with some sliced provolone, pepperoni, and saltines. This way you and Lucky can have your talk and be comfortable. She's got some homemade wine down there too."

"Where's Lucky?" I asked.

"He called a few minutes ago, said he's on his way." Go ahead downstairs, Phyllis is waiting for you, go. I'll send Lucky down as soon as he gets here."

As I stepped through the doorway, something made me reach out and pet the mutt as I walked by, when, holy shit! You'd of thought Godzilla had just gotten a tetanus shot in his butt!

That little bastard lunged at me with the ferocity of a lion! I recoiled my hand with lightning speed and surprised myself in doing so. "Calm down, Fluffy!" I snapped back, backhanding Vernon in the arm for having such a stupid dog and, also, well mostly, because I was embarrassed that it scared the living crap out of me.

"I'm sorry, Nicky!" Vernon said, petting him way too fast. "He likes you, he just doesn't know you well enough yet! Here, rub his belly, he likes that. I'll hold his jaw."

"I'm all set. I'm going downstairs to wait for Lucky. You can rub Fluffy's ass." I headed through the kitchen and opened the cellar door.

"Um, Nicky?" Vernon said, before I went down.

"What?"

"His name is Lovey."

The start of the look that was forming on my face was quickly removed when Phyllis called my name from the bottom of the stairs.

"Nicky, come on down, I've got homemade wine! Come on!"

The cellar was dark and damp. It definitely needed

a dehumidifier, but I was glad there was no noise I had to contend with. The low light made me uneasy.

I quickly scanned my surroundings, as Phillis went on about something I didn't hear a word about. I was busy learning the layout.

There was a cheaply-made liquor bar with cheesy knickknacks on and around it. Behind the bar was a picture. It hung just a tad crooked on the outdated, brown paneling. It was a portrait of Pope John Paul II. He was dusty and dingy and I thought that was disrespectful.

An ugly couch and recliner sat in a dark corner in front of an old television set with rabbit ear antennas. One of them was broken and missing half way up. It had aluminum foil twisted around it to make up the missing piece. And, across the room in the other far corner, was a door. A plain door. A low-key and inconspicuous door.

It may have been my imagination, but it looked like it was cracked open about an inch or so. It was hard to see from where I was, no matter how much I squinted.

"Nicky, sit down," Phyllis barked, pulling out one of the two folding chairs from under the bridge table.

"Do you want some cheese and pepperoni? Here, here are some crackers. Pour some wine. Help yourself!"

"No thank you, Phyllis. I don't drink. Well, hardly anyway."

"Okay, I'll save this for Lucky. He won't say no."

As she pushed aside the gallon jug of red wine, I saw her eyes quickly shift to the door at the back of the room. Then back to the table again. It was so fast, but I saw it just the same.

I sat down and reached for the saltines and made myself a cheese and pepperoni mini sandwich. "You need a drink to wash that down," she barked again. Everything with her was with a bark.

"I'll run upstairs to the kitchen for some ginger ale for you. You like ginger ale, don't you, Nicky? Lucky should be here any minute."

Her walk to the stairs was brisk and deliberate but not before glancing again at that cracked-open door in the dark corner of the cellar again. She ran up the stairs, like she'd done it a hundred times before.

I sat back in my chair and decided whether to put the whole thing in my mouth or bite into the saltines and spew crumbs everywhere including my lap. I ended up just putting the whole thing in my mouth and hoped for the best.

My text alert dinged on my phone. It was Jessie Jayne. The text messages between us went like this.

"Nicky?"

"Yes, Jessie?"

"Nicky, I.."

"What's wrong, Jessie?"

"The District Attorney just announced that the rape charges against Councilman Woodrow Woody Getz would be dropped due to a lack of evidence."

"What? Why?"

"They said Getz has an alibi. A witness says he was with Getz at the time of the assault. He's going to walk, Nicky! He's going to walk and do it again to someone else!"

Just then, upstairs, I could hear Fluffy yipping and yapping, nonstop, loud, like a nervous wreck. It reminded me of the movie with that dog in the well and the crazy guy creepily telling his kidnapped victim that "It rubs the lotion on its skin or else it gets the hose again, and now it places the lotion in the basket!"

I texted Jessie back. "That's awful Jess, I have to go though. I'll talk to you later for sure, bye."

With an overfull mouth of crackers, pepperoni,

and mozzarella cheese, I looked up to the sound of the dog's bark as it increased in volume.

The cellar door abruptly opened and feet rapidly ran down the steps faster than was necessary. I squinted through the dim light. It wasn't two feet, but four, and they were at the bottom step before I could reach for my .380, sitting secretly in my ankle holster on my right leg.

"Don't move a fuckin' inch, asshole, the massive figure said with authority, while the other figure came into view and was quickly on me before I knew it. They were both holding pieces, either 9-millimeter or .45 caliber semi-autos by the looks of the large frames.

It was Mountain and Crazy Carlo, the two renegade soldiers from the New York outfit. They were the same two scumbags that tortured Bobby C and left him for dead, vowing to do the same to me, if not worse.

Staring into two gun barrels, I spoke first, looking directly at Mountain. "I guess you didn't find that kicking your teeth out and leaving them imbedded in the guardrail on 95 very funny, did you fat ass?"

Crazy Carlo found the handgun on my leg and lifted it high in the air for Mountain to see.

"Look Mountain, this guy carries a Walther PPK! The same piece that James Bond carries! Here you were calling him the Lone Ranger, and he actually thinks he's fuckin' 007! What a douche bag!"

"Sit him down," Mountain said. "He moves a muscle, shoot him! But for fuck's sake, I hope he doesn't! I don't want to kill him just yet. I've fantasized about the different ways we are going to torture the shit out of him. You guys want to hear some of them?"

"Hell, yeah, I do! Tell me," Crazy Carlo said, like a five-year-old brat whining to his mother for a Happy Meal. Mountain grabbed the other folding chair.

"I guess Lucky's not coming, huh?" I said to the big ape, as he spun the chair around and sat on it backwards, facing me with a big grin on his giant, foul face.

"Boy, you're ugly," I said. "It looks like you fell out of the ugly tree and hit every branch on the way down."

Shut up! Carlo responded. "Mountain, you want me to whack him a few times?"

"No. No whacks, nothing. Nothing but torture." He then laid his gun on the table, smiled, and rubbed his hands together. "Hey funny man," Mountain said.

"Yes?" I replied.

"Do you believe I bought a fuckin' book on torture and sick shit? Just for you, Nicky Mancusso. Just for you! Ready to hear about it?"

"Well, do I have a choice? Because if I do, I vote no. I want to be surprised instead. I love surprises."

"Sorry, no vote, asshole," Carlo said, standing just to my left while Mountain leaned forward on the front two chair legs, leaving the rear legs inches off the floor. Mountain began again.

"First, we are going to strip you, bare ass naked, and lay you on your back, spread-eagle, and tie you tightly to stakes in the floor, at the wrists and ankles with piano wire of course."

"Then, with the piano wire tied like a hang man's noose around all joints, every time you flinch, even just a little, the piano wire tightens and cuts deeper and deeper into your flesh until it reaches wrists and ankle bones."

"Finally," Mountain continued, louder and more excited this time. "Now, this is the best part! It's fuckin' great! Did you see the movie Braveheart? Do you know what disemboweling is? I'm a fucking expert on it now!"

"In the movie, William Wallace, some bullshit fuckin' hero, got disemboweled in front of a crowd of people in the town square! They used to do that shit all the time back in the day! Wait, but wait! There's more!"

"Are you still with me, Lone Ranger?"

"Oh, I'm still here, Lumpy. Can't wait to hear the ending," I said, with a smirk on my face and a twinkle in my eye.

"Okay, well this is the best part! You're gonna love this! So..., I sit on your legs, with an extra sharp skinning knife in hand, you know..., the kind they use to field dress or gut a deer with? I make an incision, only about an eighth of an inch deep, just under your balls. Not to kill you or anything." He looked over at Carlo for a reaction.

"Then, I slice around your penis and up through your belly button all the way to your breast plate on your chest." Mountain continued to rub his hands together with a look of sheer delight.

"Wait," I interrupted. "I get anesthesia through this lovely procedure, right?"

Crazy Carlo snapped at me right away. "Shut up and listen, smart ass!" He was dying to clock me, but fat ass had already told him he couldn't.

Mountain started talking again where he left off.

The dude spit while he spoke which totally disgusted me.

"Anesthesia? Oh, no! You're wide awake through this, trust me! I kind of skin you alive, if you will! I slowly skin both sides of the incision and peel away the fascia and connective tissue as I go! I create an opening big enough to expose your pile of intestines, or your bowels, if you want to call them that!"

I nodded my head in agreement. "Hmm, interesting, Lumpy. Please continue."

"Then, then, are you ready for this? I wrap my hands around, lift up, and place the whole kit and caboodle of intestines out and onto the floor right next to you, still connected! Is this un-fuckin' real or what? And because they are still attached to you, you stay alive! You get to stay alive and watch the whole fuckin' thing! But don't forget, don't move or the piano wire will tighten and sting you like a thousand yellow jackets!" With a big, ugly, toothless smile, he waited for a response.

I sighed a long sigh before speaking.

"Are we at the end of the story yet? I gotta be somewhere in a few minutes," I said, with eyebrows raised and a look of boredom.

"Shut up, you Providence prick," Carlo said,

back-handing me across the right side of my face! It stung but didn't bother me much. Growing up in the boxing gym as most kids in my neighborhood did, it taught me how to take a punch, never mind a slap like that.

"Ya know," I said, shifting my weight in my seat from right to left, eyeing Mountain's .45 caliber on the bridge table next to the cheese and crackers. "Your mother's gonna wash your mouth out with soap, if you keep up with the bad language. By the way, where's Lucky? He's missing this cool story," I said, before Crazy Carlo stomped on my foot with the heel of his. With all his might I should add. Now *that* was bothersome.

Mountain immediately hollered through a phlegm-filled throat, never bothering to clear it. The guy was disgusting. "Don't hurt him, Carlo! Not yet! I'll cut this short so we can start the process."

"Where was I? Oh, yeah," his mucus-filled voice continued. "So, once the bowels are in a pile, laying on the floor off to your side, we leave the room. Oh wait! I forgot to tell you this part! Crazy Carlo bought eleven rats from a guy, who knows a guy, who owns a pest-control business. These rats were caught under a slaughter house in the Bronx where they slaughtered horses to make dog food. These rats are dirty, smelly, and nasty, with thick leathery tails covered in fine strands of peach fuzz rising from the tailbone. Their tails are almost as long as their matted and slimy bodies, which is fuckin' awesome!"

"But best of all, Carlo hasn't fed these plague-carrying vermin in almost two weeks, and the exterminator guy had them a week before that! He didn't feed them a fuckin' thing!"

"The rat owner said he started with twelve rats, but one was weak, so the rest of them started to eat that one alive before the guy caught on and removed the half-dead, putrid critter. These skeevy rats are literally starving to death, so we can't wait to feed them! On you, Lone Ranger! On you!"

"Before we trap them in there alone with your naked ass, we will set up cameras, so we all, including you, can watch them scurry over to your reeking innards and sniff, nibble, sniff, nibble, begin to bite, and eat your fuckin' intestines! Mmmm!"

"You can watch closely, as one or two beady-eyed, wet-nosed and long-toothed scavengers go into a frenzy after they taste a delectable strand of bowel, then squeal for joy, attracting the rest of the rats to fight for a spot."

"I wonder though, Lone Ranger, if you shit yourself, do you think the crap will squirt out of the nibble holes of your intestines? I don't think they'll care about a little shit, do you? And of course, you know that with a hoard of sewer rats fighting for the same food source, at least one rat will climb up onto your rib cage, sniff down into your open body cavity and just, hop right in, with you viewing the whole thing! Fuckin' gross, huh?"

I sat back in my chair, took a deep breath, and stared him down for a few seconds, then, through my nose, I exhaled a long and controlled lungful of air. "Mountain," I said, then took another slow and meaningful breath of air. "I got two things to say."

He leaned back, smiling, placing all four chair legs back on the floor.

"Go ahead, Mancusso. I'm listening."

"First of all, I gotta say, you are one sick bastard. Ugly as sin *and* sick. And I'm not just saying that. Did your mother not give you enough attention as a fat little kid?"

"And, second, can I have a glass of that homemade wine to wash down the saltine crackers that I ate earlier? It's been distracting me from your story. Because of that, I missed a few parts, can you tell me the story again?" *Whack!* The butt end of Crazy Carlo's gun landed squarely on my left temple. It hurt, but I didn't show it.

"Is that all you got?" I asked. *Whack!* This time one caught me across my mouth and left jaw. That one hurt more, but I didn't show that one either. I just spit out a clot of blood which landed between Mountain's feet and onto Phyllis's nice nineteen-seventy era flooring.

"That's enough!" Mountain hollered, his smile gone from his face. He was all business now. "Let's go! Carlo, cuff this poor bastard, and throw him in the back of the van! Let's go see if he squeals like a girl! I know you were disappointed when you couldn't get Castratoro to beg, but I think this guy won't disappoint you. Come on!"

"I'm not going," I said, quietly and confidently.

"Fuck, yes you are!" Mountain barked loudly back, as he stood from the chair, tipping it over as he did.

"Nah," I replied, "Not unless I can bring my friends."

"Friends? What friends? He chuckled, pulling up and straightening his pants."

"The ones standing behind you!"

Mountain spun around, fast, as Crazy Carlo did the same. In fact, they both almost got their legs tangled up with each other's as they turned, too quick and off balanced, squinting into the darkened corner of the cellar where that cracked-open door was. Only, the door was now opened wide and standing shoulder-to-shoulder in front of it were two rows of men. My men. Armed to the teeth and ready for bear. The look on the New York stooges was priceless.

Just like a high school yearbook photo, in the first row, left to right, stood Micky Carella, aka Friday Night, Mike Tessoni, aka Iron Mike, and Tony Canatta, aka Jackpot.

In the second row, stood Tommy Gaglione, aka Gags, Brandon and Brendon Sacoccia, and of course Nunzio Sabatoni, aka No Neck. My whole crew was there, except for Bobby Castratoro, aka Bobby C, the standup guy that wouldn't break while those two brilliones tortured and left him for dead.

"Lay the gun on the table, Carlo, now!" ordered Friday Night, with a small arsenal trained on the two of them. Crazy Carlo complied.

"Jackpot, get the other gun from the table! Brandon and Brendon, pat them down. Real good."

"Will do, Friday," Jackpot replied. The Sacoccia

brothers remained silent until Brandon found a knife on Mountain which was hidden in his waistband. He held it up high to show the rest of us. It looked like a deer hunting knife with a hook on it for skinning.

"You okay, Skipper?"

"Yeah, thanks, Friday. Do what you have to do, don't worry about me."

My guys threw Mountain and Crazy Carlo on the ugly couch after securing their hands with wire ties. I attended to my blood-filled mouth with Phyllis's napkins. *Oh, Phyllis, I forgot about Phyllis!*

"Hey Phyllis!" I hollered, as I walked over to the bottom of the cellar stairs. She already had the door at the top opened and was peeking out like a *fica nasa* while holding her pooch like she was protecting it against something evil.

"Come on down, Phyllis." She came halfway down and squatted on the steps, holding the railing to steady herself.

"Did I do good, Nicky?" she asked, with Mountain and Crazy Carlo looking up, perplexed. She glared back at them, giving them the *malocchio*! (the evil eye).

I lowered my voice. "You did real good, Phyllis."

She lowered hers. "I did what you asked. I left the bulkhead open so your guys could come through the back of the cellar before any of you got here. They were so quiet, Nicky. I never knew when they were there and when they weren't. But there is one thing we don't understand?"

Climbing the stairs and forcing her up with me, I answered her as we both got to the top. Vernon was waiting in the kitchen for us.

"What's that? What do you want to know?"

"How did you know those two guys would show up here? You told us to let them in when they did, but how did you know they would?"

"Wait, hold on one minute." I walked back to the top of the cellar stairs and yelled down. "Guys, I'm going now! I'll be at the location!"

Two or three of my crew members hollered back among quiet conversations down below.

"Right! Alright, Skipper!"

As I stood at the top of the stairs, I was right to expect an attempt by those two sickos at having the last word.

"The guys in New York aren't going to be happy with this treatment!" Mountain announced, in a confident, phlegm-filled and bellowing voice. "You guys..." I turned, grabbed the cellar door handle, and slammed the door behind me in mid-sentence.

"Alright, Phyllis, I'll answer you both. How did I know that Mountain and Crazy Carlo knew that I'd be here? Because the meeting I was having here was with your brother, Lucky. And your brother Lucky is a degenerate gambler that would sell his soul to the devil. I knew he would rat me out to the very people who put his head in a vice and popped his eye out."

I continued. "A degenerate gambler will do anything for money to place the next bet. That includes selling out the very guy that saved his butt! I knew Lucky would get word to those goons and collect the reward on our heads. He's probably halfway to Foxwoods Casino by now. That's why I contacted you two and gave you the opportunity to redeem yourselves. You're not stupid. You knew that when Bobby C got out of the hospital, you two would be the first two on our list to visit. You knew that we would figure out that it was you both that gave up Bobby's Sunday morning bakery routine, allowing him to get snatched up!" I headed to the door.

"So, Nicky, so we are good now? Did we redeem ourselves? We are moving to Arizona, so we are good?"

"Leave tomorrow, Phyllis. Send for your things

later. You, Vernon, and Fluffy. And don't ever come back. Get it? Ever, *capische*?"

"We get it, Nicky," Phyllis answered, with Vernon nodding like a bobble head on the dash of a '55 Chevy.

"Thank you, Nicky. Just one more thing before you go?"

"What, Phyllis?"

"It's Lovey, not Fluffy.

EIGHTEEN

What a day, I thought, tilting my head back against the headrest and searching for a good song on the radio. I did that whenever I needed to decompress.

"In the Air Tonight," by Phil Collins. *Oh God, So sick of that song. I even heard Collins in an interview say that he hates the song now too, because everybody and their mother plays it in the commercial world. Me too.* I kept searching.

I noticed I always hit the radio scan button hard when I disliked a song. "It Keeps You Runnin'" by The Doobie Brothers. *Ugh... Worse. Change it.* I did.

"What's this? Sounds like the Grateful Dead. Don't know the song, just grateful that they are. Now I was a little pissed. *Change it.* I pushed hard on the radio button.

"Delilah," by Tom Jones. *Here we go. Love it and it never gets old.* I was already at the Pink Pussy Cat and not happy. It was always the way. Two or three sucky songs and just when a good one comes on, I get to where I'm going and gotta cut it short. I could have sat in my truck until it was over, but I would never do that. I don't know why. I guess it just seemed goofy.

I shut the truck off and hopped right out at the good part. Jimmy the Weasel was standing outside the main door, staring me down like he knew I was coming.

"Nicky," he hollered, in a whisper. "The boss wants to see you."

"That's why I'm here. Excuse me." He stepped aside.

Although we were both Captains, he always treated me with more respect than I gave him.

As I entered the Cat, for the ninth time it seemed, my eyes had to adjust to the dim lighting. The place was packed at that hour; it always was after 8 p.m. That's when the guys who had wives and girlfriends got there, completing their relationship duties before going out with the guys afterwards. More and more though, the club was becoming filled with women. That would have been unheard of twenty-five years ago.

The music was loud as usual. Because of the high

number of girls on duty between 8:00 and closing, they usually had two dancers on stage at one time, sharing the same stripper pole. The guys liked that. I couldn't care less.

As luck had it, Star was up there accepting a sawbuck in her G-string. Even from that distance, I could always distinguish between a ten and a one or a five, depending on what the customer was wearing. In this business, I'm a profiler.

This particular guy had straight-legged jeans on, with Timberland-type work boots with dirt smudges on them. He wore a forest green Carhartt shirt and a worn-out Buck Fever hat, unraveling at the brim. He gave the dancer a ten, while the guy with the expensive looking, three-piece suit next to him gave out only ones. It was always the way.

The song ended, and Star and the other dancer picked up the bills on the stage floor. Ones and tens. She saw me and worked fast, probably to speak to me.

I nodded for Scammy to pour me a club soda, so I could stall a minute before heading to the way-back to see Boss Santini. I tipped back the glass, and before I knew it, she was standing right next to me.

"Mr. Mancusso, how are you, Nicky!" She looked amazing. I couldn't get over how much she looked like her sister, Moon. Except without the knife blade sticking out of her right eye socket.

Her body was still fit. The outfits she chose were beyond sexy, and her makeup was fantastic. Similar to Alex's, but for some reason hers looked sexier, while Alex's was classier.

Last week I think I would have chosen Alex over Star but not now. It must be because I disliked her now. Finding out that she was wearing a wire in my presence knocked me for a loop and made her ugly to me.

When my attorney, John O'Brien, gave me that gizmo for my keychain that detects bugs, I totally forgot about it and never thought I'd need it. Especially for my therapist, the one person I was supposed to trust with my deepest secrets.

The wire she wore probably had an entire task force of FBI agents listening eagerly on the other end. In this day and age, I can't believe they use their limited number of resources on organized crime instead of concentrating on the Taliban or Iranian sleeper cells right here in Providence.

I know they are trying to pinch me with the death of my best friend, Carmine Torro. They have his kid, Nicholas, stashed away in an army camp with the hopes he'll crack and testify against me. We had to get to him before they do, godson or not.

"I'm doing well, Star. You look great as usual. How is Nicki?"

"She's growing like a weed. Next, I'll be fighting off all the boys," she giggled, leaning in to kiss my cheek, then wiping the lipstick off me with her glitter-speckled thumb, while fixing my collar as she pulled away. It felt like a thousand eyes were on us, and I noticed my face getting hot.

"I gotta go, Star, I have a meeting. I'm sorry."

"Again? Are you avoiding me, Nicky? Why can't we hang out? I thought by moving back to Providence from L.A. would bring the three of us closer. I really thought you cared about me after you did what you did for me. You never forgot about me! Sending money now and then showed me just how much you cared! When Nicki was a little girl, I talked about you all the time! And when I dated, which wasn't very often, I compared them all to you!"

"You are a standup guy, Nicky, and you saved my life. I will never forget that. Can't you find just a little time for me in your life?"

We just stood there, looking at each other for what seemed like an eternity! I didn't know what to say!

Her eyes were leaking, like Grace's does when she's hurt.

"Nicky! The boss is waiting," the underboss hollered, coming out of nowhere but immediately commanding my respect. Bruno Lucetti had to have seen Star's watery eyes and that was unacceptable. Especially for a man in my position. She was a stripper, and I was a "made man" with my own crew. I could never forget that.

"I have to go, Star, I'm sorry. It was nice talking with you. I'll see you soon."

Leaving her standing there was cruel of me, I know. But what was I supposed to do? I never looked back. I couldn't. So, I headed to the back room with Bruno in tow. Anytime the boss wants to see you is nerve racking.

When you really know you have to worry is when you enter a room escorted by your friends, and upon entering you quickly realize that there is a tarp or rolled out heavy-gaged plastic under your feet. That's when you know. That's when you quickly say a Hail Mary prayer and hope they don't miss the shot to the back of your head.

When we entered the first back-room, there was the usual one or two card games going on. Mostly all degenerate gamblers or suckers. The house always wins. Always. But they should know better. They should know that they cannot be the one to beat the odds and break the house's bank. It's not going to happen.

A state worker once told me that the biggest sucker's bet with the worst odds was with the government, The Rhode Island Lottery. He said you have a better chance of being struck by lightning, not once but twice! Friggin' crooks.

Bruno and I meandered through the card tables, as I made my greetings to mostly the old timers. I knew them all.

Ronnie T was standing watch outside the boss's door and knocked when he saw us. He stuck his head in, pulled it out just as fast, and opened the door for me and the underboss. I brushed up against him as I went through the doorway.

"Hello, Ronnie, how's everything?"

"Great, Nicky. And you? Heard you got some New York troubles."

"I'm good, Ronnie. Yeah, nothing we can't handle." He closed the door behind him and stood guard at his post and was still there when we emerged thirty minutes later.

NINETEEN

Running anywhere, especially in public just wasn't my style. A cool, deliberate walk, scanning my surroundings and never drawing attention to myself was my way. But if I wanted to catch Jessie Jayne before she left for her shift, I had to hoof it.

The traffic wasn't bad, so I made it to the hospital fairly quickly. I usually used the valet parking when it was open, it was. I threw the guy a sawbuck and trotted into the unit entrance.

Two cops were standing in front of the elevator, as I excused myself and pushed the up-arrow button. The door opened right away, so I hopped in and pushed the door-close button as they eyed me down until the seam in the door was closed tight.

Arriving around the corner from the nurse's station was good. That gave me time to peek to see if my friend was there, and if not, walk the corridors and zone in on each room as I passed. As room 4450 came into view, a tiny busy-bee of a person flew from the room and almost ran me over. It was Jessie Jayne.

"Hey, where are you going like a bat out of hell?"

"Nicky! What are you doing here? I'm off in 5 minutes! You're just in time. I haven't had supper yet and I'm starving. We can play some gin rummy!"

"I wish I could, Jessie. I just stopped by to give you this. Here."

The tiny package I had tucked inside my jacket pocket didn't come out easily. Plus, I was embarrassed to give it to her, so I was all thumbs. She took it from me with a confused look on her small face.

"I am in such a hurry, I can't even wait to see you open it, Jess!" I backed up slowly then picked up speed. "I'll talk to you soon! I hope you like it!"

She just stood there, holding the Italian marble, mother of pearl rosary beads. The short note read, "My mother gave me these prayer beads for my First Communion, they were hers. I hope you like them."

As I made my way past each floor, I imagined Jessie on her lunch break, sitting by the Virgin Mary statue in the hospital garden area, and maybe holding my mother's beads between all her ten fingers. It was a nice thought.

I arrived back at the club well past its closing time of 2 a.m. The Pink Pussy Cat's neon sign was dark, but its silhouette was still visible. It looked strange without all the cars that usually parked tightly together to squeeze them all in at once.

On a good night, there could be as many as fifty girls on duty, either walking the floor or dancing on stage. The large numbers attracted patrons from as far away as Boston and Hartford. And, our prime-time girls were knockouts. Every one of them. The house mom made sure of that.

You could be as dumb as a stump, but if you were a knockout, you got hired. Of course, it was really just paint and paper.

Sometimes I'd see the girls arrive before their shift and literally not recognize them until they emerged from the make-up room downstairs, going from plain Jane to Carmen Electra.

I drove to the back of the lot and Friday Night's '69 Camaro came into view. Then I noticed Iron Mike's Chevy 4x4 parked next to that. All the doors opened up when they saw me, and members of my crew piled out.

"Hey, Skipper," Friday whispered, always the one to greet me first. Jackpot didn't say a word, just emerged from the passenger seat and handed me a hot Dunkin Donut's coffee, still steaming out the cup's lid hole.

Tommy Gag emerged from the back seat with No Neck Nunzio following behind, pushing his way out of the 2-door, and plopping both his size fourteens onto the parking lot pavement.

God he's big, I thought.

Brandon and Brendon stood by Iron Mike's pickup as Mikey walked over to me. It was dark but over his shoulder I could see a figure in the passenger seat of the 4x4. It was still.

"Hey, Nicky," Mikey whispered, raising his eyebrows only a bit, then standing by me in a protective posture. I just nodded.

The night was nippy, so I peeled the plastic thing back on my coffee cup and warmed my lips. As some steam escaped, I took a long sip of the hot coffee, while raising my eyes to the silhouetted sign before the night's sky.

"You guys have something to show me?"

Friday night gestured with his head. "This way, Skipper." I slowly followed.

As we walked, Brandon and Brendon opened the Chevy's door and helped the shadowy figure out and over to our direction. As they got close, Friday Night spoke.

"Does this guy look familiar, Skipper?"

"Does he look familiar?" I replied. By now the rest of the guys, Jackpot, Gags, and No Neck had surrounded us.

"Yeah, Boss. Do you know this guy?" Jackpot asked, "Does he look familiar? After all, you told me to bring him here tonight. Well, here he is!"

I took a few steps forward. "I don't know. Let me look into his eyes. Brandon and Brendon, hold onto him tight, don't let him fall. Bring him close."

With my arms spread wide, I ordered the boys to bring him in closer still. So close that I wrapped myself around him in the gentlest bear hug.

"How you doin', Bobby C, alright?" I released the hug as not to hurt him.

Enduring a buckwheat and living to tell about it is unheard of, and I wasn't going to push his luck. A 22 caliber bullet up the bum isn't strong enough to travel clear through the body, and that's why it's done. The bullet bounces off organs and spirals through intestines and bone, before the victim bleeds to death internally in a lingering and agonizing demise. Not to mention mentally.

Bobby was thrown into a dumpster and left to rot to death for days. Trash and feces were thrown on him, while maggots crawled over his entire body while botflies searched for orifices to enter through. Not to mention the mice and rats that lived in those things.

"I'm doin' okay, Skipper. I'll be back in action in no time, I promise. And, Skipper? Thank you for finding me. And thank you for having Friday take care of my family. I mean..."

"Okay, that's okay, Bobby. Now don't go gettin' all mushy on me. And don't wear yourself out, either. You gotta be gettin' back soon. I just wanted to see you, that's why I had the guys bring you here tonight. This is where it happened. Do you remember? Here is the dumpster!"

I pointed to our right, just feet away. "This is where those two scumbags from New York put you, Bobby Castratoro, a soldier in our family! Our family!" I wasn't whispering anymore. "Right here, here in this dumpster!"

Jackpot and Iron Mike shined their flashlights on it, as I walked over to it, kicking the side twice with the front of my shoe. The putrid stench of it infiltrated my nose and hit me like a ton of bricks! It stunk like hell, forcing me to take a step back!

As some loose rust tumbled off the side of the dumpster and on to the dark ground below, I remembered Moon sitting there in her Beamer that night years ago.

She was tucked way back in the shadows, hidden beside that smelly thing. At first and for days after, I thought she was her twin sister, Star. Gorgeous, sexy, and quite dead. The dagger sticking in her eye socket told me she was. But that was a long time ago. I kicked the dumpster again!

"Bobby, come here. Come stand by my side." He looked surprised, not moving a muscle. His eyes shifted right then left, then back to me.

"You want me by that obnoxious remembrance, again, Skipper?"

"Just come stand by me," I said, waiting patiently, as he slowly began to come. I gave a quick look to Friday Night who gave a look to Jackpot, who was already in motion, coming towards us with the rest of the crew right behind him. Brandon and Brendon were moving fast, maneuvering past Iron Mike and No Neck Nunzio.

Still weak, Bobby spun around and braced himself for whatever was coming next.

Brandon flew past Bobby, sidestepped me, and ran into the dumpster with both hands, stopping himself at the last minute as he collided. He reached for the lid with his right hand, then with his left. He then lifted the dumpster's heavy metal top, all dented and hinged.

As he pushed the weighted cover up and open, the putrid smell became stronger, especially from the wind that was created when Brandon flew it open. An enormous *clang* emanated through the night's quiet, forcing every one of us to look to our surroundings as not to get caught.

"You have something to show us?" I asked Brandon, as he waited for his orders.

"Yes, we do, Skipper. Take a look inside."

"Bobby, look with me," I said, taking his arm and guiding him over the side to peek into that disgusting bin with me.

As we both leaned over the side, my crew surrounded it where they could, and slowly lit up the inside with their phones, as the contents began to slowly come into view.

Trash, I didn't recognize, lined the inner walls

along with solidified ooze sticking to the tops of the sides. The stench was nauseating.

A pile, of what looked like bathroom trash, was strewn in one corner. It contained bunches of toilet paper and used and bloody sanitary napkins. So disgusting.

Then my eyes locked on a bizarre sight, and what a sight it was.

There, among the food and feces, were the forms of two bodies, like fossils, outlining the contour of something that didn't belong. But these two things belonged, in my book anyway.

There, lay the bodies of Mountain and Crazy Carlo. And they were very much alive!

Friday and Jackpot bellied up to the dumpster and leaned over the edge. Iron Mike leaned into the thing while turning his head away from the smell.

"Hey boys," I said, talking down to the contents of that dumpster. "How you guys doin'? Everybody alright? Need anything? Wait! You're all set! There's a half-eaten egg salad sandwich right there by your ear, Mountain, get it! Oh wait! You can't! You got buckwheated!"

The rogue wise guys had their eyes opened so

wide, I thought they'd pop right out of their ugly heads! Yet they blinked! Slowly!

"Yeah!" Jackpot hollered. "A buckwheat? You shoot a small caliber bullet up someone's hiney, not to kill him right away of course. You guys taught us that!"

Hey Crazy Carlo, I'll bet Mountain's breath smells like ass, with his lips up against your open mouth like that!"

"All right, that's enough," I said. "We are not animals, remember that." "You're right, sorry Skipper," Jackpot replied.

Bobby C leaned over the edge for a better look just in time to see two maggots crawl across Mountain's rosy-red cheeks!

Bobby spit a baseball player's, between-the-teeth, squirt-spit on the two of them. "This is how we do it in Providence, scumbags. Next time stay in your own neighborhood. I told you you'd pay for what you did to me!" He spat again.

Bobby shakily turned to me, while Jackpot held his arm. "Thank you, Skipper. I don't know what to say."

"Say you'll get better, get stronger than before, and take care of your two families. *Capische*?"

"*Capische*, Skipper."

"Good, now I have one more thing to show you. Mikey, you got that thing?" Iron Mike emerged from the back of the crew. He'd retrieved a sack, while I took another sip of my hot coffee. The sack was strewn over his left shoulder and looked heavy, but it was hard to tell how much because of Mike's size.

"Step back a little, Bobby. Let Mikey through." Iron Mike approached the dumpster and threw the sack from his shoulder and onto the edge. Brandon stepped forward with a large hunting knife.

"Hey fatso, remember this? It's mine now, thanks!" One side of the blade was shiny and the other had serrated teeth that were chipped in spots. Brandon proceeded. He stabbed the point into the sack and ran the shiny edge up the burlap bag until it opened up and revealed its contents.

There, lying across the top side of the dumpster was the pervert that molested my friend Jessie, councilman/political bigshot, Woodrow "Woody" Getz. He looked as though he was drugged. Maybe he was?

He looked good actually, although his penis wasn't where it should have been. Not between his legs anyway.

Hanging out the side of his mouth were two

shriveled up testicles and a pathetic little penis lodged between his false-looking and over-polished and glistening teeth. The message was sent.

Friday nodded to Mikey, and Woody got tossed over the edge and onto his new friends. A muffled thump was followed by a long and drawn-out moan from one of the two original tenants down below. Mountain, I was guessing. Then Iron Mike dropped the heavy lid onto the dumpster with a tremendous clang! And that was that. Case closed.

The boys helped Bobby C into the Camaro, and we called it a night.

On my way home I couldn't help but think of Jessie. I had to keep my distance from her now. She'd never see me again and would never know why. And, my "Nevers" are forever. Because of Getz, I could never be seen with her again.

The lights were still on in our bedroom, as I pulled into my driveway. That was weird. Grace goes to bed early, so I was surprised and apprehensive. I went in slow but loud enough as not to startle my wife.

"Is that you, Nicky?" The television was on, probably its usual chick flick or tear jerker. Grace would make me watch them with her and would laugh when I cried. I wanted to cry when she laughed.

"It's me, Grace." I turned the sound down just a little as I passed the new 60-inch Sony.

"I thought you were all done with late night work, Nicky? Didn't you promise me that?"

Just then, Grace's chick flick ended and the nightly news began.

"Good evening! I'm Amy O'Brien, and this is News Team Twelve! Tonight, we have two top stories. Our first begins with a story of a fire at the Fort Devens, Army facility in Waltham Mass! Our, I-Team reporter, Sandra Swanson has the full story!"

"Uh oh," I whispered, with my back to Grace.

"Thank you, Amy, Army officials have confirmed that a fire erupted tonight in an isolated barrack at the Fort Devens Army Camp in Waltham Massachusetts! Police say that one man is dead. Sources say that the man was a witness in an organized crime investigation. The fire is listed as suspicious and the Massachusetts State Police report they will investigate. Back to you, Amy!"

"Thank you, Sandra. Our next top story begins with a heartbreaking tragedy in the city of Warwick. Night Beat reporter, Susan Young, has the story.

"Hello, Amy. I'm here in Warwick where police say earlier tonight a psychotherapist named Alexandra,

"Alex" Elizabeth Pearlmutter, was coming home to her East Side apartment when two masked men emerged from the shadows, subdued her, and sporadically poured an acid like compound on her face and body.

"Doctors at Saint Mary's Hospital said they had never seen such a brutal marring. They expect Miss Pearlmutter to survive; however, she will need countless surgeries and will most likely be horrendously disfigured for the rest of her life. Her neighbors heard nothing and could only say how beautiful she was. Police have no suspects at this time."

"Back to you, Amy.

"Thank you, Susan. This is Amy O'Brien, News Team 12, and we will be back, after these messages.

"Oh, my God, Nicky! That's terrible, just terrible! That poor girl! Those sick, sick psychopaths, that's what they are! What is this world coming to?" Grace lowered the television's volume more before continuing. "I'm glad you are home, Nicky. Where were you tonight? It's late!"

"It was business, Grace. Just usual business stuff."

"What kind of business"?

Sitting at the edge of the bed, still looking at the television, I fussed with a knot while untying my shoes as fleeting images of Star, Jessie, and the sexy and stunningly Alex passed before my mind's eyes. A harder tug on the lace released the knot and washed their faces away.

"I had to meet two guys from New York tonight. Then when we were about to leave, a third guy, a local politician showed up. I had to take care of all three of them before I left. I owed them that. "A promise is a promise and my word is good. You know that."

"I hope they know that, Nicky."

"Oh, they know it."

"What type of business are the New Yorkers in? I'm glad you took care of them."

"What type of business are they in?" I looked back at the television and didn't take my eyes off it as I spoke. "Um, they're in, they're in garbage, Grace. All three of them."

She reached for her end table lamp and clicked it off. "Oh, that's nice. And I'm glad you took care of them. You always do the right thing. Well, goodnight, Nicky."

"Of course I took care of them. It's the Italian way." *It is the La Cosa Nostra way,* I thought. *This thing of ours.* Goodnight, Grace. I love you."

"I love you too, Nicky. My endearing husband."

Bobby DePalo is a retired entrepreneur who built and led his company for 37 years before selling it and stepping back in 2023. In 1999, a life-altering accident left him paralyzed—an experience that initially set him back but ultimately fueled his determination. Against the odds, Bobby rebuilt momentum and scaled his business to a point of lasting pride.

He is the author of several books, including *A Promise*, *More Promises*, *The Code*, and *Making Bones*. His most popular and deeply personal title, *Kantfly: A Paraplegic's Story*, is a self-help memoir that offers an unfiltered look into his private journey and resilience.

www.ingramcontent.com/pod-product-compliance
Lightning Source LLC
LaVergne TN
LVHW010651110826
845149LV00014B/3036

* 9 7 8 1 9 6 8 5 4 8 5 6 8 *